FREE INDEED

One Woman's Victory Over Lesbianism

WALNUT STREET U.M. CHURCH
P.O. Box 509
Chillicothe Ohio 45601

FREE INDEED

One woman's victory over lesbianism

Barbara Swallow

as told to Terry Murphy

EXODUS

FREE INDEED

Copyright © 2000 Barbara Swallow and Terry Murphy

All Rights Reserved. No part of this publication may be reproduced, stored in a retrieval system or transmitted in any form or by any means—electronic, mechanical, photocopy, recording or any other— except for brief quotations in printed reviews, without the prior permission of the author.

This story is true. However, some names and identifying details have been altered to protect the privacy of the individuals involved.

Unless otherwise noted, all Scripture quotations are taken from the *New King James Version.* Copyright © 1979, 1980, 1982 by Thomas Nelson, Inc., Nashville, Tennessee. All rights reserved.

Cover photos by Rick Soto, courtesy of RiCarte's Photography, Albuquerque, NM

ISBN: 0-931593-58-1

Published by Exodus International North America

**For more information or
to order additional copies, please contact:**

Exodus International North America
P.O. Box 77652
Seattle, WA 98177 USA
(206) 784-7799

Printed in Canada

To my loving husband, Ronald. You are a man of God. You prayed for our marriage when you didn't even know how to pray. I thank God for your love and faithfulness in times of great stress.

Isaiah 6:8 says, "I heard the voice of the Lord saying, 'Whom shall I send, and who will go for Us?' Then I said, 'Here I am, send me.'"

Ronald, this is how you have lived. Thank you for listening to the Lord.

■ ACKNOWLEDGMENTS

To my husband, Ronald:
Thank you for your courage and prayers. For your crazy sense of humor that made me laugh when I was feeling down or discouraged. I love you very much. Thank you for trusting in God.

To my friend, Jeanne Cook:
You have been a mentor to me, an inspiration and an example of godly womanhood. Thank you for being there, even when you didn't understand my struggle. You are a faithful friend.

To Terry Murphy:
Thank you for your steadfast patience and persistence when I was tired after long hours of looking back at my life. Thank you for being the expression of me on paper that I could not be myself.

To Glory Christian Fellowship:
Thank you, Pastors Joe and Nancy Cangolosi, and David and Margi Wintermute, for all your love, prayers, and constant support.

FREE INDEED

To Exodus International North America:
> Thank you to the staff and board of directors for the encouragement to complete the work that God had started. You have been a safe place to grow and change.

Dear Reader,

What's normal, anyway? Our ideas are pretty well fixed by our early experiences in life. Before we have had an opportunity to compare our lives with others, we've drawn conclusions about our families, our life and ourselves in general. A mother doesn't "normally" require sexual favors of her daughter. A father is "normally" able to treat his daughter as female. Parents don't "normally" buy and sell love and acceptance. But these were all part of my life and I knew nothing different until I was a wife, a mother—and a practicing lesbian.

I knew what gratification felt like, but not satisfaction. I knew how to fight for acceptance, but not how to find it. I wanted to be loved, yet I never seemed able to earn it. I didn't know what was wrong in my life. I was just unhappy. (I can only find one picture of myself smiling as a child!) Year after year, plowing the hard-packed ground of approval, toiling for love, I wearied of life itself.

Can "normal" change? It did for me. After many years of trying to make life work the way I thought it should, something began to happen to me. Slowly but surely, bit by bit, normal began turning inside out. Now, forty-some years later, I finally know what love feels like, what it means to be abundantly satisfied, and what it feels like to be whole.

Your friend,
Barbara Swallow

■ PROLOGUE

I pulled the covers over my eyes, pressing them as tightly as possible around my ears. My knuckles were white, and terror gripped my chest, making it almost impossible to breathe. They were coming again. Heads, with faces. Screaming, without sound. Coming at me, out of the darkness. Closer and closer. Faces with hollowed-out eyes that glowed red and yellow. Hollow features on animated, mask-like faces. Blotched and streaked with white and black, with reds and blues and yellows... like war paint... some heads crowned with wild, electrified hair.

In an inexplicably calm voice, I called, "Ma, Ma," again and again. I didn't scream. My chest screamed. My lungs screamed, but my voice would not. I pushed that scream down... down.

Finally, someone called back to ask what I wanted. "I'm having a nightmare." But it was a lie. I was wide awake and the screaming faces were still coming at me and disappearing over my head.

"Well, then come down here."

So, down through the terrible darkness, I picked my way to my parents' bedroom. I was five years old, but I was so small for my age that I could not yet reach the light switches, and asking to have someone get up and switch them on for me would get me into trouble. So, gripping the high banister, I crept down the stairs in that frightening, thick darkness. As the stairs curled to the left, I lowered myself on my bottom, one step at a time, to keep from falling. The steps narrowed sharply on the railing side as they turned, and my feet were unsure of themselves.

In my parents' bedroom, my mother called me to her side of the bed and held me very close. She wore no clothes. Now it was even harder to breathe. Her breasts were so large that my face was always in them. She made me suck them as if I was nursing. *But I'm too old for that!* I thought. She took my hand and moved it down, down to her private places while I nursed. And she wouldn't let me go.

Every night, I went up to that attic room with my brother and sister to go to bed. Back up to that attic room painted dark, dark green. Green walls. Green ceiling. Every night, when all was very dark and very quiet, when everyone else had gone to sleep, I lay awake. And the faces came back.

If I couldn't stand the faces, I would call for my mother again and go down to her. But I hated what happened when I went down to her; so most nights I just pushed that scream down deeper and deeper, and waited for the dawn to chase the faces away.

Only then would I sleep.

■ PART ONE

Going Down to the Tomb

■ CHAPTER ONE

What led me to the conclusion that no one loved me as a girl? Disturbing as it was, my relationship with my mother was only one of many contributing factors. As a child, the only times I remember being given individual attention by my mother occurred when I played the male role in her bed. Unconsciously, I began to accept the idea that my value rested in my sexual capabilities. Perhaps, if I could function as a boy, I would be loved, and would prove myself to be of some merit.

I don't know what caused my mother to do what she did. She has passed away now, so I can only speculate. I do remember, however, noticing a change in my mother's personality after one particular event. Perhaps her inability to finish grieving over that incident is what led to such incongruous behavior and neglect.

When I was around four years old, I distinctly remember my mother going to the hospital to have a baby. I remember just as distinctly that she came home without a baby. No one ever explained this, and I must have simply assumed she and Dad had decided not to have a baby after all. Still, I could not understand why Mom got so angry whenever we tried to play with that lovely, double-sized baby carriage in the basement.

Mom changed after that; Dad changed, too. All of our lives seemed to take a turn for the worse from then on.

Within a year, we moved to a house in the country. Our house had an attic room that, for some reason, my father decided to paint dark green. It was out from the depths of those dark green walls that the faces began to come.

By this time, Mom spent most of her time in bed. She stopped getting up every mealtime to feed us. She would get up to make Dad's dinner, but the only times I remember having the table set and food fixed for us kids were once or twice a year when the extended family gathered for some holiday. Even then, it was traumatic for my mother because she hated entertaining. My sister, Pat, who was then about eleven years old, pretty much took care of my brother and me. Mom was too depressed to get involved.

My father, who had always been distant, became even more detached. When he came home from work, he sat behind his newspaper while he ate his dinner. No one spoke. On Saturdays, he spent hours in the back of the house, taking care of his yard and his chickens. If we got within three feet of him back there, he would say, "That's close enough. Now go away."

On Saturdays, when my mother was well enough to go out, she and Dad went into town for a shopping excursion. We kids went along, but we had to stay in the car where we waited, sometimes for hours, while they shopped. Eventually, they would return to the car to unload their packages, and to give each of us a box of animal crackers. Then the two of them would go into the diner while we waited in the car again, until they finished eating.

We had no central heat or hot water for the first two or three years we lived in that house. Bath water had to be heated on a big black kerosene stove in the kitchen. If the weather wasn't too cold, we got a bath about once a week. My brother, Charlie, and I were

CHAPTER ONE

only eighteen months apart; when we got too old to share the tub, only the first one to get into the bath got clean water.

Despite these unpleasant circumstances, I have some happy memories of playing with my brother. When we were still only four or five years old, the two of us would wake up about five o'clock every morning and forage in the kitchen for a piece of bread or something else to eat. Then we'd go out in our underwear and explore for the whole day. I remember a pear tree down the street where we usually went to get some fruit for a treat. There were other fruit trees and berry bushes all over the neighborhood, so whenever we got hungry, we were usually able to find something to nibble.

There was a garden in our backyard, but if we were caught taking anything from it, we found ourselves in serious trouble. In part, I think my parents were worried about its stability, due to the fact that it was built over the cesspool. However, I believe they also sold their vegetables to make extra money, and they were more concerned about having the produce depleted. I remember canning vegetables every year and taking the jars down to the cellar. Those vegetables were never served to us children, except for holidays. My father, however, regularly ate them for his dinners.

Charlie and I took in stride the danger of stealing things out of the family garden. In fact, we saw it as a challenge. Carrots were out of the question, as they left a conspicuous hole in the ground when pulled. However, string beans were easy to sneak, so we took plenty of them whenever we could. Once we had our fill, off we sped to go exploring, or playing cowboys and Indians, or football with the neighborhood boys when we got a little older. We stayed out all day. No one cared whether we came or went, and there was no reason for us to go home for lunch—there wouldn't be anything to eat, anyway. Frequently, we stayed out until dark, returning home only if we decided to put on some clothes.

I owned a few dolls and I remember setting them up at their appropriate doll tables, with chairs, cups and saucers, giving the appearance that I was playing with them. But it was only an illusion.

FREE INDEED

Instead, I joined my brother and his friends in their activities. If anyone asked, however, it was easy enough to pretend to give the dolls some attention.

There was one doll, however, that I particularly loved. She was an ugly old wooden doll that had been given to me at the same time I received a lovely modern doll. At first I played only with the modern doll, with her painted hair and eyes that opened and closed. But one day I came home to find the dog had chewed all the toes and fingers off the wooden doll, and my attitude toward her totally changed. I wrapped up the poor maimed thing in bandages, and nursed and cared for her exclusively from then on. She was so wounded that my heart went out to her.

Perhaps, even then, I already identified with her pain.

By this time, I was beginning to notice how different we were from other kids. When our cousins came to visit, they were bathed, dressed in clean clothes, and had neatly combed hair. Although I tried to convince myself they were my "rich" cousins, I dreaded the thought that, when I started first grade, I would find out that other kids were dressed in clean clothes, too. I was afraid that I would be "different." As it turned out, I was right, and just as my cousins had teased me, so did the kids at school.

I used to love it when my aunt came to visit from the city. She spent what seemed to me like hours combing out all the knots and tangles that had been left unattended in my hair. This personal attention, although such a small act of kindness, was a welcome luxury to my self-esteem.

Because of my small size and our lack of a kindergarten, I began school in the first grade at the age of seven. We were new to the Long Island community, and I was treated as an outsider. My appearance and lack of personal hygiene caused me to be teased unmercifully, and playground time at school became a nightmare. I spent most of recess avoiding the mocking of my classmates and creating a sanctuary for myself by befriending the teachers. Although I earned good grades at school, my efforts went unnoticed

CHAPTER ONE

at home. My mother never looked at my report cards. She just signed them and sent them back.

On the other hand, even though my brother was a poor student in school, my mother continually doted on him. She made countless trips to school to find out what was wrong with his grades. All her attention went to him. From my perspective, being a boy certainly seemed like a better fate than being a girl.

Our family was ostensibly Catholic, which gave the other children another reason to keep their distance. The whole community was Protestant, and being Catholic was considered heathen and idolatrous. Fortunately for me, even though none of us had any real relationship with God at the time, we did participate in the Sacraments, and when I was around eight years old, I received my first Holy Communion.

That night, when those faces that had harassed me for two and one-half years came back, I said "no" to them. I told them, "You may be scaring me, but Jesus is in me now, and you can't touch me." And they left me!

Taking communion, I had been told, meant that Jesus was on the inside of me. But how did I know, at that age, that having Jesus inside me gave me authority over those faces? I can only believe that God, in His tender love and sovereignty, sent me help before I even knew how to ask for it. In any case, after two and one-half years, with nothing left to drive me out of my room, the visits to my mother's bed finally ceased.

Between the ages of nine and thirteen, I began to be the "son" my father had always wanted. Dad and I never developed any real closeness, but I was able to spend time in my father's presence by helping him with manual labor around the house. My brother was never interested in the things my dad wanted him to do. So when Dad began fulfilling his life-long dream of building a house, I became his co-laborer. I did carpentry work and mixed concrete and hauled cinder blocks right alongside of my dad. He even got into the habit of calling me "Bob" instead of Barbara.

FREE INDEED

I remember building a cesspool with him when I was twelve years old. The fifteen-foot deep cavity was dug into the earth with a narrow three-foot opening that widened out below. With my father down the hole, I was responsible for lowering an empty bucket down for him to fill with soil. Then I hauled the full bucket carefully up through the narrow opening. I say "carefully," because if I had accidentally hit the side with that full heavy bucket, the whole thing would have collapsed on him and buried him alive. It says something about my abilities, I suppose, that my father would have entrusted this job to a twelve-year-old girl who was still very small for her age.

By that time, I was living in jeans, T-shirts, and sneakers. There was no dress code, but this was in the early 1950s, and most girls my age still wore skirts to school. I no longer thought of myself as a girl, however. I preferred thinking of myself as just a neutral sort of "person."

Everything seemed to conspire against me being happy as a girl. When I had been a "boy" for my mother, she noticed me. When I shared in the "manly" duties around the house, my father had occasion to talk to me. When I played with my brother and his friends, I was happy. When I was thirteen, my older sister got married and moved out. I was then selected, as the remaining female child, to take over all the housecleaning. My brother was never required to help with housework. Along with everything else, I was even expected to clean his room. In school, I was required to dress like a girl and act like a girl. And yet, while trying to play that role, I was cruelly and definitively rejected. At home or at school, playing a girl's role didn't get me praise; it brought me slavery and torment.

And so, the stage was set. I was ready to be noticed. But who would pay attention to me? It wasn't long before I stopped trying to be the girl God had created, and chose instead to seek another path toward acceptance, love and belonging.

■ CHAPTER TWO

Throughout my teenage years, I did outwardly what girls are supposed to do. Other people expected me to act like a girl, so I dated and participated in "girl talk." It kept me from looking, on the outside, as different as I was feeling on the inside. Yet, I really didn't want to be a girl. I felt like a boy.

Boys were fascinating to other girls, but not to me. I already knew what boys were like, inside and out. But girls were intriguing because I didn't understand how they thought. Girls were mysterious. What made them so soft and gentle? Every aspect of my personality that craved nurturing was drawn to the hope of being cradled in some form of sweet female attention.

Then Charlotte came into my life and she became my first real friend. Our backgrounds were similar. She was new in town, also from the "wrong side of the tracks," and therefore an outcast. I turned out to be the first person in school who bothered to talk to her, and immediately we became fast friends.

I had no experience with developing any kind of relationship with another person, either male or female. I had no relationship with either of my parents. I was neither used to having anyone care for my needs, nor had I any experience in caring for another person's needs. By the time I was nine, I was on my own. I learned how to keep myself clean by watching how other kids did it. No one paid attention to what—or even if—I had eaten.

And now, all at once, someone else was interested in what was going on with me and in what I had to say. It was new and exciting. Feeling another person's attention was a delicious and satisfying experience, and my thirsty soul soaked it up like parched desert soil soaks up the summer rains.

Charlotte began to talk to me about boy-girl relationships. They didn't sound all that exciting to me, but it was wonderful having someone confide in me and trust me. She would tell me how much she liked this boy or that, and how she would like to kiss them. All I could think was, *Why?* It didn't seem intriguing to me at all. I already realized that I preferred girls' company to boys'. Nonetheless, I pretended to be excited with her.

Charlotte and I spent a lot of time together. Sometimes when I stayed overnight at her house, we would sit out in her barn and smoke cigarettes. Because it was cold, we would sit close together. I liked the feeling. We talked and shared, but I could not stir up the feelings for boys that my friend had. More to the point, I couldn't explain to myself why.

Strange things kept happening to me, in those early years, which fed and magnified my confusion. I remember waiting for someone to pick me up after a Brownie meeting when I was eight years old.

"Little girl, what's your name?" asked a teenage girl as she approached me.

"Barbara," I nervously answered, starting to walk away.

"Don't run away. Come over and sit with us."

Over on the lawn, several girls were sitting in a circle. Some were my age; others were older girls I had seen at school. They seemed to be having fun, so I moved a little closer.

CHAPTER TWO

As soon as I was within reach, the girl who had called me began gently stroking my leg. I jumped in surprise, and quickly began walking away. I never waited around for a ride again. I preferred to walk the one and one-half miles through the dark in order to get home. I hated the dark, but I was even more afraid of those girls.

They were always around at school, talking about me behind my back and staring at me. I remember once, in sixth grade, needing urgently to go to the restroom during class. I tried to wait until recess, when there would be a lot of girls in the bathroom—and no danger, I hoped, of unwanted attention from any of the girls from the lawn. Minutes passed, but it was no use. I couldn't wait. I'd just have to risk it. I raised my hand to be dismissed.

At first, the restroom seemed all clear. If I hurried, I thought, everything would be all right. But just as I came out to wash my hands, two of the girls I had hoped to avoid walked into the room.

"Hi. What are you doing here all by yourself?"

"I was just leaving." I tried to move quickly past them, but I didn't make it.

One girl grabbed me by the arm and said, "Wait a minute. Let's be nice and friendly." She pushed me up against the sink and pressed her body close to mine.

Giggling, the other girl said, "You know you like it, so stop trying to get away."

The terrible thing was that, deep inside, a part of me agreed with her. But I was afraid that someone would walk in and see what we were doing. I started to cry. I was so confused inside. I wanted to resist the feelings being stirred up in me, but they were so strong.

This is crazy, I thought. *Let me out of here!*

Finally, I managed to break away and I rushed back to the classroom. Behind me, I could hear the other girls laughing uncontrollably. I strained to regain my composure before I walked through the classroom door, terrified that everyone would somehow know what had happened just by looking at me. No one seemed to notice anything when I re-entered the room, but I felt awful inside.

FREE INDEED

It was hard to forget the feeling of excitement in being close to that girl. What was happening to me?

Another day, I picked up one of the "true story" magazines all the girls seemed to read. Maybe I could learn what all this boy-girl stuff was about. I read a story about lesbian lovers, and at last I seemed to have the answer. *I've felt this way!* I said to myself. *So THAT'S why I feel so different!*

And so it was, at age thirteen, that I labeled myself as a lesbian.

Throughout the next few years, similar incidents occurred, though always in secret. The same girls who pressed themselves on me in private totally ignored me when I was in the hallways. I only seemed to exist when they wanted to touch me.

When I was in seventh grade, another one of those girls from the lawn tried to befriend me. After school one day, we were supposed to be playing baseball for intramural sports. Carla had forgotten to bring her shorts, so she asked me to walk to her house with her while she changed clothes.

Her father was home, and I could immediately see that he was drunk. When we walked into the house, he said some really ugly things to Carla. I was shocked, but she just smirked and whispered, "Don't get too close to him, or he'll touch you."

I tried to stay in the hall while she changed, but Carla dragged me into the bedroom. "Are you crazy? You can't stay out there alone!" I didn't want to watch her change. I knew I'd get those crazy feelings again. I was afraid to be in there with her, anyway, because of incidents like those in the school bathrooms. So I stayed by the door, worried about getting too close.

"Don't worry," she assured me, "I won't do anything here. 'He' is home."

I didn't know whether I felt relief for being spared, or disappointment at being neglected.

Carla changed shorts a few times, asking me which shorts looked best. It was very difficult for me to watch her change. Finally we agreed on a pair of white ones, but by that time, I didn't much

CHAPTER TWO

care anymore. I just wanted to get out of there. Opposite desires were battling within me. To make matters worse, after all that, when we finally got back to school it was too late to play ball!

The next sequence of events are rather unexplainable, and don't make much sense, even to me. Nevertheless, they happened. At the time, being so inexperienced and uninformed about what was normal, I failed to see anything contradictory in them. Now I understand them better, in light of what I've learned about gender confusion and how it affects adolescents.

Charlotte, my one straight friend, went with me to the movies one day. Three boys were sitting a few rows in front of us. Charlotte was always on the prowl and she wanted to try to pick them up. I agreed to help, on the condition that I could have "the blonde one." The boys needed little encouragement, and soon they moved back with us. Then came, for me, a clumsy and very uncomfortable experience with kissing. Afterward, the boys walked us both to the bus stop.

Ronnie, my "date," was quiet but I felt remarkably comfortable talking with him. He gave me his school football button and told me we would see each other again some time. Once on the bus, I told Charlotte that this was the boy I would marry some day. Charlotte thought I was crazy, of course. I was only thirteen, for heaven's sake! How could I know whom I was going to marry? Unknown to any of us, my statement was prophetic. And, strangely enough, Ronnie got on his bus and said virtually the same thing about me: "Someday I'm going to marry her...."

But it was four years until we saw each other again.

Meanwhile, in ninth grade, I went to a different junior high school for a year. It was close to my mother's job, so I rode with her to work and walked the extra four blocks to school.

Just outside the grounds, a group of three or four girls sat smoking every day. The first few times, I simply walked by them. Eventually, I began to say "hello" as I walked past each morning. Finally, after four weeks, I stopped and asked if I could bum a cigarette.

"Sure, come join us. You have plenty of time before the bell rings."

They were right—I had an hour to kill. And from that day, we became "morning friends." I should have been suspicious of the quality of their friendship when they ignored me in the halls just as the girls at the other school had done. But I had grown accustomed to that kind of treatment.

On rainy or winter days, when it was too cold or wet to go out at lunchtime, the school had music piped into the gym. Anyone was welcome to dance until class resumed. Sometimes one of the girls in my "morning" group approached me, twisted my arm and dragged me onto the dance floor. Whenever slow music was played, she pressed herself close to me. If the music sped up, she just walked away, leaving me standing alone. It was bad enough that people were already staring at us because of the way we were dancing. But it was even worse to be discarded by her, right in the middle of the gym, in full view of everyone. I was so ashamed that I wanted to die.

One of those rainy days in the gym, a student named Mike asked me to dance. He looked like a weasel, but I said "yes," figuring it would keep me busy and prevent that girl from getting close to me. I was wrong. She came over and cut in. Mike told her to get lost, but she wouldn't take no for an answer. She began to shove him and blows were exchanged. Suddenly I had a girl *and* a boy fighting over me—talk about gender confusion!

As the school year progressed, I began spending more time with Charlotte. After school, I'd get together with her and her boyfriend, Doug, plus two of his friends. Occasionally, when Doug's mother wasn't home, we went to his house, where Doug and Charlotte would take the opportunity to make out. This made things a little awkward, because that left me with two guys and no idea what to do. After a while, one of Doug's friends began making advances toward me. I let him kiss me. I didn't do it out of desire; the activity simply provided me an excuse to stick around. I would have agreed to anything short of sex in order to stay close to Charlotte.

CHAPTER TWO

During the summer between ninth and tenth grade, Charlotte and I did a lot of bike-riding and swimming. We worked in her father's azalea nursery, pulling weeds for sixty-five cents an hour. Charlotte would flirt with the guys who worked there, and I would pretend to laugh with her. But I felt jealousy building up inside me. There wasn't anything I could do about it, but I didn't like seeing her with anyone else.

In high school, I caught up with the girls from grade school who had been such a problem for me. Now, there seemed to be a kind of "knowing" between us. We never said it to each other in so many words, but each of us knew that the others were lesbians.

It seems that once a person yields to a certain sin or weakness, he or she becomes a magnet for anyone else who has succumbed to the same sort of urge. People with similar behavior patterns manage to "find" each other and hang around together. People who are into drugs have no trouble finding those who have drugs to give them. People fascinated with pornography always seem to find themselves surrounded by people who encourage that activity. Either misery really does love company, or we all just like to be found standing next to someone whose lifestyle doesn't make ours look so bad.

The summer before tenth grade, Charlotte and I were riding our bikes home from the beach. Some girls in a car wanted to pass us, and Charlotte would not move out of the way. I knew it meant trouble. They were mean, and as they finally drove by, I recognized the girl from the gym.

Sure enough, when we got about two miles down the road, I spotted their car parked by the side of the road. I tried to warn Charlotte, but it was too late. They came flying out of the bushes and pushed us off our bikes. The girl from the gym yelled, "Don't touch that one," meaning me.

I tried to drag them away from Charlotte, but the girl from the gym kept pulling me away and laughing. They blackened Charlotte's eye, punched her repeatedly and tore her clothes. It was terrible, but there was nothing I could do to stop them.

Fortunately, a car pulled up. Some guys got out and broke up the fight. Charlotte was angry with me after that, because she didn't believe I tried hard enough to stop the other girls from hurting her. Her father was so angry that we weren't allowed to see each other for a while. She started hanging out with other people and I started "seeing" other boys.

Charlotte and I remained friends, but for a while, our relationship cooled.

■ CHAPTER THREE

Eventually, Charlotte became the connector between Ronald and me. After her friendship with me was restored, she was determined to get the two of us together. She found out that Ronald was working at the supermarket in town, and she dragged me into the market under the pretext of getting some vegetables. Later, we found out that he liked to roller-skate on Friday and Saturday nights.

The following weekend, I talked Charlotte into going with me to the skating rink. Before we left, Charlotte and her mother fixed my hair and make-up. Thanks to their efforts, I looked quite respectable, and off to the rink we went. Once we located Ronald, Charlotte dared me to ask him to skate with me. Much to her amazement, I did. Ronald and I spent the rest of the evening together.

I invited him to the beach the following Sunday, but he declined. "I'm going to church that day," he explained.

I was stunned. An eighteen-year-old boy who wasn't ashamed to admit that he went to church? I couldn't believe it. Even then, a hungry place in my heart was already yearning for God. It was stirred anew when I saw Ronald's faith.

FREE INDEED

I didn't have the boldness to ask where he attended church, but armed with the name of his nearby hometown, I forced Charlotte to join me on a quest. The following Sunday, starting at one end of the town's main street, I decided we would visit one church at a time until we found him. Fortunately, we hit the right church on our first try. My mouth dropped open in awe as I saw Ronald up front, wearing a white robe and reading the day's Scripture passages.

Ronald had some questions about my availability to date; by this time, I was unofficially engaged to a man of my parents' choosing. Initially I had gone along with the engagement; marriage to Tom—the man they had chosen—sounded like freedom to me.

Since the moment I had become a woman in their eyes, my parents' neglect of me had been transformed into constant scrutiny of my movements and acquaintances. They seemed to have an all-consuming need to know who I was with and where I was going. The connection between puberty and pregnancy had never been explained to me so, as far as I was concerned, these sudden restrictions made no sense.

In fact, around the age of fifteen, puberty had taken me completely by surprise. My first period was a terrifying experience; I had no idea what was happening and thought I was dying of some terrible disease. Somehow my mother heard about my trauma and tossed some supplies to me without explaining how to use them. She never talked to me at all about the whole menstruation process. Eventually I learned from friends that monthly bleeding was normal, but I began to deeply resent the fact that this process was being pushed on me, whether or not I wanted to be a girl.

I had no particular loyalty to Tom; he was nothing more than a ticket out of this new restrictive life imposed by my parents. So, according to my conscience, I had no problem with dating Ronald. Meanwhile, I can only say that my attraction to Ronald was a sovereign move of God on my behalf, preparing the way for my deliverance long before I had any idea there was something from which to be delivered. To a certain extent, I think I was being drawn

CHAPTER THREE

to Jesus *in* Ronald. Somewhere, deep inside, my heart recognized and wanted the Savior who led him.

Psalm 37:23 says, "The steps of a good man are ordered of the LORD." God loves us before we love Him. Even when we are still unbelievers, God is busy ordering and preparing things, so that when we turn to Him, He already has our deliverance underway. What an incredible miracle it was to have this same wonderful man waiting to hold me close to his heart, almost forty years later, when at last I emerged from all the lies and confusion.

Ronald and I began to see each other every evening and all weekend long. We went to his church together, and had dinner with his family on Sundays and Wednesdays. Immediately I felt like part of his family. He took me to meet his aunts and uncles and his grandparents, who were warm, loving, and accepting of me. At last, I felt that I had found the family I'd been looking for all my life.

Ronald proposed to me on our way to the Christmas dance during his senior year in high school. When we told his folks, they were thrilled. They simply asked us to wait a couple of years before we actually got married. My parents, on the other hand, weren't quite as enthusiastic.

When I told Mom the good news, she shouted, "I'll engage *you!*" and she stormed away. My father said nothing at all.

"What about Tom?" Mom shouted later. "You're supposed to marry him when he comes home on leave from the Air Force!"

"I've already written to him," I explained.

That didn't solve the problem. They both made it very clear that they did not want me to marry "that guy" (as they referred to Ronald) because—of all things—he wasn't Catholic!

Oh, right! I thought. *You don't even go to church, and you're upset about which one Ronald attends?*

By this time, I had quit school and Ronald was set to graduate in June. Since neither of our families was ready to see us get married, we decided to elope. We began saving money for our wedding and honeymoon. Ronald, newly drafted into the Army, was to report for basic training the next October, so we planned for a September ceremony.

We saved and prepared all through the summer. Every weekend, we went out all day on Saturday and Sunday. That way, when we eloped and didn't come home, no one would wonder where we had gone. We drove from Long Island into New York City, or for long rides in the country. We made a point of not returning home until the wee hours of the morning. I bought new clothes and put them in a suitcase hidden in the trunk of Ronald's car. When the day came, we left for a "date," as usual. A Methodist minister in Maryland married us on September 28, 1955. It had only been ten months since our original skating date.

Unfortunately, after we had planned and scheduled everything for the elopement, my mother was diagnosed with a tumor and quickly underwent a hysterectomy. Only five days after she returned home from the hospital, Ronald and I left to get married. Everything had been scheduled for months, and we couldn't change our plans. But my mother took it as a personal snub, feeling deserted and ignored. The entire episode created terrible turmoil in my family.

Immediately after our wedding, Ronald went into basic training while I stayed in a hotel room in my hometown and worked at the phone company. He was seventy-five miles away, and if I wanted to see him during his limited leave time, those miles would have to be crossed. My work schedule had to be coordinated with bus schedules, and it only allowed for one day off at a time. It was a huge obstacle to try and arrange for someone to trade days with me so I could have two days off in a row. Soon we conceded that we could not realistically expect to see each other more than one day a week. Charlotte convinced me that it would make more sense for me to live at home until Ronald's basic training was over. So I moved back with my parents for a short time.

When I arrived, my mother assumed that I wanted out of the marriage, and excitedly began to talk about an annulment. I explained to her that I was only home temporarily, and I did not

CHAPTER THREE

want to leave Ronald. This indignity, on top of being deserted after her hysterectomy, was the last straw. My mother did not speak to me again for three years.

Ronald and I had been married about a year when our son, Ronald Jr., was born. Things were hard for us financially; my mother-in-law took care of my new son for a time so I could go back to work.

While riding on the bus to my job, I met a woman named Marla. She was one of about five women who rode the bus with me to work. She was friendly and saved a seat for me each morning. After about two weeks, she started coming to my workplace with little gifts of candy and some snacks for break time. Eventually Marla began buying lunch for me almost every day. "You can use the extra help financially," she explained.

Meanwhile, just before Ronald's basic training was over, the military doctors discovered that he had recurrent mastoid infections, which affected the area behind his ears. They promptly released him from service. Fortunately, it didn't take him long to get a better-paying job, so I was able to quit my job at the phone company.

Marla was disappointed that we would no longer see each other every day. She suggested that we could get together in the evenings or on weekends, whenever Ronald was working. And so began a relationship that would span the next sixteen years. It started out as a friendship. It developed into what I thought was love. It ended in disaster.

In the beginning, the friendship seemed like such a good thing. Ronald was exhausted by his new job. He got up at three o'clock in the morning, and came home at 1:30 in the afternoon. He had no time or energy left for the baby or for me. But Marla had lots of free time and lots of tender loving care to give to both of us.

She did for me the kinds of things I had always thought my mother should have done. She helped with the cleaning, and loved to take over the cooking. Finally I had someone caring for me, sharing the womanly duties of which I had grown so weary.

One day, when Marla had been helping out with Ronald Jr. and

FREE INDEED

we were both tired, we sat down on the bed to talk and catch our breath. After a few minutes, the talk slowed down and the room grew quiet. Softly and gently, Marla leaned over and kissed me. It was surprising but incredibly satisfying. It was the first time I had ever been kissed by a woman. All the passion that had lain dormant in me began to come to life and I was finally tasting what I had been resisting so long. After that unexpected encounter, I wondered why I had feared yielding to it for so long.

From that moment, Marla and I became lovers. To keep a relationship with her *and* my husband, I had to burn the candle at both ends. But I was a person full of nervous energy who never slept much anyway. Even years after the faces had disappeared from my bedroom, I still didn't sleep well. The only place my mother had ever acknowledged me was in the bedroom, and I felt I had great talent there. In my own little world inside my head, I was convinced that I could please both Ronald and Marla. I also imagined that it would take the appetites of two people to keep me satisfied.

Almost as soon as my relationship with Marla began, Ronald began tying himself up with work and union activities. He seemed to be losing interest in spiritual things and he stopped making time for God. Without realizing it, he was letting go of the very cord that had connected me to him in the first place. With Marla's help at home, things seemed to be running like clockwork; there was no worry for him there. Marla was busy taking care of me, so Ronald was relieved of that confusing responsibility. And, as often happens when things seem to be going well, no one saw any reason to ask God for advice. No one was aware of any danger. No one saw the ugly storm on the horizon. No one was prepared for its fury.

On working days, my time with Ronald was in the afternoon when he came home from work. As I recall, Ronald and I were great in bed, but we were connected only by sex. We talked about the kids, the money or the weather, but we didn't talk in depth about anything. Not being included in any serious dialogue with him made me feel like an unintelligent, unimportant knick-knack on his

CHAPTER THREE

shelf. I didn't feel Ronald saw me as capable of supplying relevant input for important decisions. I didn't see my opinions being sought out or valued. I didn't believe that I was valued by my husband.

During this time, Marla was at our house every Saturday when Ronald came home from work, and she cooked dinner for both of us. She was a great cook, and Ronald loved the attention. Then Ronald went to bed and slept while I did my housework. Since I didn't sleep much anyway, I thought it was a convenient time to get things done. When Ronald got up, Marla would still be there, and she would make breakfast for him. As soon as he left around three a.m., Marla joined me in my bedroom. We kept each other very busy in bed until around five or six a.m., when Ron Jr. would wake up.

Looking back, I wonder how I managed to keep everything together. During those sixteen years, I was a wife, mother, and lesbian lover. I took in ironing to earn money so my children could have some extras. By the time all three children were born, I was sewing and making their clothes and mine. I was, by turns, a Cub Scout den mother, an assistant Girl Scout leader, and the leader of an after-school religion class. I was sort of the local "auntie" and our house was always filled with kids. I swam, hiked, and played with my children, determined to be for them all that my parents had not been for me.

I never slept. I never stopped. It's amazing how much stays unresolved when a person never stops to examine herself. Before my other two children were born, Marla was content with sharing the responsibility for Ron Jr., coming over during the daytime to help me out. And gradually, my relationship with her became more and more demanding.

Although Marla gave me a certain amount of emotional support, it wasn't long before she started belittling my opinions and putting me down. She began to treat me with the same disregard as Ronald. Sometimes, when the three of us were together and there was a ball game on television, Ron and Marla would be on the couch, laughing and joking and enjoying the game together while I was completely left out. I felt forgotten by both of them. It was a reenactment of my fifth year of life. Then, as now, no one complained when they were in bed with me—but no one seemed to want me anywhere else.

My ideas and opinions were constantly corrected or discounted. Decisions were always made for me by one of my two "protectors." It seemed to me that both Ron and Marla saw me as a poor, foolish little thing who needed someone big and strong to take charge. So they did. I saw myself as invisible, inept, incapable. When I walked into a room, I became convinced that no one even knew I was there. Hiding in this invisibility was strangely comfortable. But I was extremely lonely, even though I was never alone.

Curiously, my life with Marla was reflective of my life with my mother. They were very much alike, and many of the things Marla and I did together were reflections of what had gone on in my mother's bed so many years ago. Occasionally, bits and flashes of those times with her would try to appear on the horizon of my memory, but I refused to look at them. I couldn't allow those memories to completely surface, because they couldn't possibly be true. It was many years before I was finally ready to look back into the faces, to look into the bedroom, and to deal with all that happened there.

Early in my relationship with Marla, I wanted to get out. I even took Marla to confession with me several times, where we made commitments to change the relationship back into a friendship. Despite our best intentions, it was too late.

Marla and I were both tremendous actors, playing our parts beautifully: she, the loving friend; I, the faithful wife. All this was going on in the same bed, and Ronald never knew anything about it. *How can he not know?* I asked myself a thousand times. I wanted him to get suspicious, to rise up and put a stop to all this madness. But he never did. We played our parts too well. I was angry with Ronald just as I had been with my father. Both men were supposed to protect me. Why didn't they?

All this time, Marla's possessiveness was growing like a cancer. When I became pregnant with my daughter Sonjia, Marla's

CHAPTER THREE

jealousy began to swell. Obviously I was still having relations with my husband, and that was a slap in the face to her.

By now my friend Charlotte was also married and living nearby. But when I tried to renew our acquaintance, Marla became very restrictive. Whenever I took a call, Marla wanted to know who was on the phone. Whenever I wanted to visit with someone outside my family, I had to limit my time with them. Marla started having some of my friends followed and harassed; she was going to make sure I wasn't close to anyone but her. In particular, she had Charlotte followed secretly.

No one believed Charlotte when she complained—everyone thought she was being paranoid. And eventually, Marla's behavior pushed Charlotte over the edge; she had an emotional breakdown and was hospitalized. Marla had successfully kept her out of my life, and she tried to prevent me from establishing any other friendships.

This was peculiar in light of the fact that, a few nights every week, Marla was with someone else. I was her primary relationship, but by no means her only one. I was jealous, too, and might have tried to control her. But I didn't have her kind of power, and I was too busy with my children to pursue any kind of surveillance. There was no way I could keep an eye on Marla and her activities when she was away from me.

As months turned into years, my relationship with Marla became more and more insane, possessive, and manipulative. Each of us had made the other partner the center of our lives. Each of us, in essence, wanted to be the other person's "god," worshiped and adored, exclusively and at all cost. Before it was over, each of us would learn much about the high price of idolatry.

■ CHAPTER FOUR

In 1962, as my second pregnancy progressed, Ronald decided that we were outgrowing our house and needed to move. I didn't really want to resettle somewhere new, but I thought perhaps it would be an easy end to the whole affair with Marla. Part of me was broken about losing her, but my situation was too crazy to continue. Both Ronald and Marla were possessive, and I was very glad for the possibility of getting out from under the authority of at least one of them. As it was, I was constantly torn between the two, trying desperately to satisfy them both.

Ronald and I moved to a house that was close to my parents, and right across the street from my sister. I thought the proximity of my family might deter Marla, but it didn't take her long to make friends with my relatives. In fact, somehow she managed to nose her way into even more areas of my family's life. Now, instead of coming over Friday nights and staying until late Saturday night, she felt free to spend the whole weekend with us. Ron never objected to this, so I didn't feel there was any alternative; I lacked the necessary courage to speak up and voice my own objections.

When Ronald and I got married, I left the Catholic Church to join the Episcopal Church with him. For some reason, Marla now wanted me to return to Catholicism. She was Catholic, and she thought that we belonged there together. Discovering that Marla was talking to me about reestablishing myself as a Catholic greatly pleased my parents. They had never recovered from my leaving the Church, so Marla became a heroine in my parents' eyes while Ronald and I almost lost our marriage over the whole issue.

Marla insisted that I talk to a priest who told me I was living in sin with Ronald because we had never been married in the Church. This, of course, meant that my children were illegitimate. Once again, I found myself trapped without choices. Religion had always been important to me. I didn't really know God personally, but I really wanted to do what was right. And here was a priest telling me what he thought was right. Why did it feel so wrong? What could I do?

I slept on the couch for about three months, until Ronald caved in and agreed to remarry under the auspices of a priest. Shortly thereafter, for the sake of keeping unity in the family, Ronald joined the Catholic Church. We also had Ronald Jr. and our new daughter, Sonjia, baptized there. In the process, Marla endeared herself to my parents for having helped their daughter to "see the light."

But Marla's impact on my marriage was another story. Ever since she had entered our lives, Ronald's interest in spiritual things had been waning. More and more, he had thrown himself into his job and, by being actively involved in his labor union, he was able to move into more powerful positions. In the union, when he saw a problem, he could figure out a solution. At home, he knew something was wrong with our marriage, but he had no idea how to fix it.

For Ronald, a family was supposed to be like the 1960s sitcom "Father Knows Best." However, "Father" didn't know much about family problems like ours. Perhaps that's why he was always running off to work and union meetings, where things were a lot more predictable: see a problem, analyze a problem, solve a problem, and you're a hero again. At home he was flying blind.

CHAPTER FOUR

I was no help; I wasn't telling him anything. For goodness' sake, what could I tell him? Yet, in some unexplainable way, I wanted him to know. I longed for him to understand not only what was going on with Marla, but what was going on with me, too. I wanted him to take care of me. I wanted him to tell me what to do. I needed him.

The truth was, I didn't understand myself. It seemed like everyone expected me to fit into a neat little package of whatever they thought I was supposed to be, but I wasn't living up to anyone's expectations. I was a square peg, and the hole I was given was round. Yet no one seemed to notice I had difficulty fitting. Try as I might to scratch and claw at that hole to get myself into it, it would not work. I didn't fit. I had never fit. It didn't occur to me that anything was wrong with me. I just thought nobody understood me.

A few months after Sonjia was born, Marla began to settle down about my daughter's arrival in our home. She came to terms with Sonjia by adopting the rather strange theory that, somehow, this baby was really *hers*. How she came to this conclusion, I'll never know, but I was glad to have her anger assuaged for a time. Perhaps thinking this way consoled Marla that I had not really been unfaithful to her. In any case, Sonjia was a precious miracle of God and before long, she became Marla's exclusive domain. Marla basically took over the care of my baby.

When Sonjia was about nine months old, Marla and I planned a weekend away in Greenwich Village. In my mind this would be a romantic and intimate getaway for the two of us, and I was ready for something romantic—there had been precious little romance since my pregnancy. Now Marla was showing some interest again, and I was determined to have a good time.

In preparation, I bought myself a new and very feminine-looking negligee for the trip. But when the first evening came, and I came out of the hotel bathroom wearing it, Marla blew up. I could not understand her anger. What had I done wrong?

In the daytime, as we roamed the streets like tourists, I wanted to be very open about our relationship. But Marla would not let me be demonstrative in public. She was terribly concerned about who might see the two of us together and what they might think. I was so tired of being secretive that, if Marla had not kept me under control, I would have just let loose and been openly gay. If there had been a march, I would have been in it. If there had been a crowd demonstrating, I would have held a sign. But Marla wanted nothing to do with public affection or openness, so I was hustled from one private place to another until it was time to go home.

Not long after that, Ronald and I began going out to wild parties and gay bars (though he never knew they were gay). When I went to these places I dressed in the only "feminine" way I understood—suggestively and seductively. When we went out, laughter and singing and merriment surrounded us. I guess all the noise helped keep us all from thinking. Why would I want to *think* about my life? It was bad enough living it.

There was no tenderness left in private with Marla, and no ownership in public. Neither did Ronald openly reveal his affection for me. All this added up to one conclusion: rejection. Rejection! I was so tired of being rejected. My husband rejected me as an intelligent person. My family rejected me for marrying the wrong kind of man. Marla publicly rejected me as a lover.

Meanwhile, she was tightening the screws of her control over me. Perhaps she felt vulnerable, having seen my willingness to be open and public about my lesbianism and realizing that I might actually have the nerve to find someone else. Maybe the negligee made her realize that I might even be attractive to someone else. Whatever the reasons, Marla's vigilance increased.

Worse yet, she began to be physically abusive, after which she used fear and intimidation to control me. I was no longer allowed to tell my husband that I loved him. My every move became suspect.

Ronald had always been a heavy drinker, but now I started drinking, too. And I drank a lot. Then, about a year after Sonjia's birth, although Ronald and I had very little intimacy, I became pregnant again. This time Marla was not willing to concede another miracle.

CHAPTER FOUR

She was furious. Ronald could not believe this was his child, either. So both of them turned away from me.

Suddenly, I was very much alone, the object of everyone's contempt. All I had done was try to love everyone. In doing so, I had lost everything. I was heartsick. Cast aside. Terrified.

Journal Entry—February 10, 1962

I feel as though I have fallen into a deep dark pit and there is no way out.

Ronald is angry. He thinks I have had an affair with the Japanese guy down the street! This is unbelievable! Even if I wanted an affair with a man, how could I possibly do it? When would I have the time? Where would I get the energy?

Ronald doesn't believe this baby is his. It makes me laugh so hard I can hardly stop! Whose baby could it possibly be? The only person I'm making love to can't even give me a baby! Ronald hardly talks to me now. He's already made up his mind. He doesn't believe me.

Marla is scaring me. She's so angry with me. She accuses me of being unfaithful to her. She says I don't love her. She is getting so rough with me.

"You've been with Ronald all along, haven't you? Even when you said I was the one you loved!"

I threw a skillet at her today in the kitchen. She just kept coming at me and coming at me; screaming, accusing.

I can't think any more. I can't remember things.

I need to ask the doctor for more of those tranquilizers today. Yes, that's what I'll do. Maybe then I can rest.

I feel so dead and empty inside.

I keep dreaming the baby is born dead.

I can't stand this any more. I think I'm falling apart. I wonder what it feels like to fall apart. I can't keep track of what I'm doing any more.

Mom came over today and told me to be more careful of what I ate, for the baby's sake. What baby? What is she talking about? Why does she think I'm having a baby? That's ridiculous, Ma! Ronald and I aren't even sleeping together!

I can't be having a baby! My God, no! I am <u>not</u> having a baby! Why is everybody so mad at me?

Where are those pills? I know I still have some left. I have to call the doctor. I have to tell him I need some more of those.

I just want to rest. Someone just take all these people away and let me rest.

■ CHAPTER FIVE

Everyone was concerned about my emotional state, and they had good reason to be. As time grew near for the delivery, the doctor decided to send me into the hospital ten days before my due date and induce labor.

Miraculously, Marie Ann was born healthy and bright. As a gift from God, she was also born conspicuously "ours." Ronald came in to see me after he had visited the nursery to see Marie Ann, and said, with some surprise, "She has red hair and blue eyes."

"What did you expect?" I asked.

"Slant eyes and dark hair." With that comment, he left.

Although his suspicions about another man had been dispelled, Ronald and I continued to drift apart. By the time Marie Ann was born, I was an alcoholic, and addicted to prescription drugs. About nine months after Marie Ann's birth, Marla stopped me as I walked to the bathroom with a bottle of Librium, my tranquilizers. I was just going to take the whole bottle and be done with it. She ripped the bottle from my hand. I was so furious that I bolted into a nearby room, slammed the door shut and locked it. I proceeded to slam

FREE INDEED

and pound at the walls, screaming and wailing like a mad woman. Everyone outside the door tried to talk me into opening the door, but I screamed and pounded for three hours.

For the next nine years, our circumstances continued to deteriorate. Marla's jealousy grew without bounds. She became increasingly abusive, both sexually and physically. She was incredibly strong, adept at creating a maximum of pain with a minimum of physical evidence. Nevertheless, I began changing clothes in the bathroom, out of Ron's sight, so he wouldn't see the carefully placed bruises.

Marla and I began to argue about the raising of my children. One time, to emphasize a statement, she went after me with a kitchen knife. She also threatened me verbally. More than once she told me, "If you aren't careful, your children might not come home from school one day. Maybe someone will find them dead in the woods. How would you like that?"

I was no longer allowed to sign Ronald's birthday cards, "Love, Barbara." Marla threatened to tell Ronald about our relationship if I did. "If you're not careful," she assured me, "you'll not only lose your children, but your husband as well."

One winter night, Marla asked me to go with her to her aunt's house. We drove out into the country for miles in the darkness until a driveway finally appeared out of nowhere. After we pulled up to a large sprawling house, Marla stopped the car. "Get out and go ring the bell," she ordered. "See if she's home."

"No! I'm not going to the door. I don't even know the woman."

But the next thing I knew, I was shoved out of the car and the door was locked behind me. As I neared the front door, I heard a low growl at my elbow. I ripped open the storm door and jammed myself between it and the large wooden door. A huge German shepherd had my coat sleeve between his teeth. Shaking with fear, I screamed, "Help me!" and pounded on the door with all my might.

Suddenly, the door flew open and I fell inside. A woman spoke to me in some foreign tongue and then in English. "Who are you?

CHAPTER FIVE

Are you crazy?" She pulled me inside, closed the wooden door on the vicious dog, and began yelling for someone to lock him up.

Marla appeared in the hall. Her aunt started shouting at her. "She could have been seriously hurt or killed! Are you crazy?"

"*I* know she could have been hurt. I wanted to make sure *she* knew."

The woman took my coat and gave me a glass of brandy to stop me from shaking. In the moments that followed, I determined never to doubt Marla's threats again. She had made her point.

■ PART TWO

Rising from the Dead

■ CHAPTER SIX

Sometimes a situation can look like it is getting worse when it's actually getting better. A new difficulty developed which looked like "just one more thing" with which I couldn't cope.

Ronald Jr. was now fifteen and we suspected that he was experimenting with marijuana. He was growing distant and aloof.

At this time, all three of our kids went to the folk masses at our Catholic church, while I attended the more traditional masses on Sundays. Ronald Sr. was not going to church at all. One day, I went to the folk mass for a change of pace, and noticed Ronald Jr. and Sonjia up with the folk group. When Communion time came, neither of them went up to receive.

"Sonjia, why aren't you receiving Communion?" I asked after Mass.

"Ronald doesn't, so why should I?"

I turned to Ronald. "Why aren't *you* receiving?"

"I don't want to. Besides, I don't even believe in all this stuff."

I was aghast. I certainly wasn't proficient enough in spiritual matters to feel comfortable discussing doctrine with him, so I sent him to talk with the priest.

FREE INDEED

Ronald Jr. was already playing guitar with the folk group, and soon the priest got him involved with teaching religion to some of the younger kids in CCD, the after-school religion class. After the school year was over, all the kids who had helped teach were invited to go on a retreat together. A priest, a nun, and a married couple who were born-again Catholics were leading the retreat.

As soon as Ronald walked back through our front door after the retreat, I knew that something had changed. Now I was sure he was on drugs—nobody could be that happy naturally!

"Don't worry, Mom," he chuckled. "I'm not high. But we had the greatest time! When Chuck and Mary began talking to us about Jesus, they talked as if they really knew Him *personally.* Later, when they asked if any of us wanted to receive Him into our hearts like they had, fifteen out of the seventeen of us who were there said 'yes!' They told us about being baptized in the Holy Spirit, and we wanted that, too."

His voice grew even more excited as he continued. "Mom, it was tremendous! After they prayed for us, we all just lifted our hands and began to worship Him. Then the most wonderful thing happened. Just like in the book of Acts, in the Bible! My heart was so full, I just thought I'd bust wide open. I had to tell God how much I loved Him, but there just weren't words to say it. So I opened my mouth, and my heart began to pour out words I'd never heard before. Somehow, I knew that those words were expressing exactly what I wanted to say to God."

I felt like I was in over my head. My son was talking about something way beyond my understanding. When he left the room, I called the church.

"Don't panic, Mrs. Swallow," a nun tried to comfort me. "Everything is okay. The kids are all going to a prayer meeting next week, and you are welcome to come join us to see what this is all about, if you'd like."

I joined Ronald Jr. at the prayer meeting. There they were, all the kids on the floor, sitting cross-legged, with their hands raised in

CHAPTER SIX

worship. This was no "kid" thing. They were really worshipping God and thoroughly enjoying it. They weren't throwing prayers in His direction, wondering whether He'd heard. They were communicating with God, having a two-way conversation with Him. And it looked so easy for them. I had always worked so hard in prayer, throwing up cries for help. I had begged, cried, repeated words over and over that I'd been told would please Him. I'd never been sure that He heard, or that He intended to do anything about my prayers. Yet these kids knew. They were very sure indeed.

I wasn't the least bit hesitant. *I* wanted this peace and comfort with God, too. *I* wanted to be able to talk to God this easily. "Lord, I want this joy, too," I silently prayed, almost afraid to hope.

I had never really experienced joy. I had laughed at jokes and funny stories during parties, but as soon as the joke was over or the party was done, the laughter was gone. I took pleasure in doing certain things, but when I was finished "doing," the good feelings vanished. These kids carried this joy with them all the time.

I prayed to experience the happiness I saw in the kids. But there was something in the way. Whatever efforts I might make in my spiritual quest would have to wait for now. The years of sexual abuse with Marla had led to endometriosis. I was scheduled for a hysterectomy. And I was very much afraid.

As the surgery approached, even Ron Jr.'s new joy became a source of fear for me. I did not share his confidence in God. I had developed a terrible fear that I was going to die on the operating table, and if I did, I was certainly not ready to face God with any confidence at all.

My son tried talking to me the day before I left for the hospital. He told me not to be afraid, because God would make all things work for good for me. "And even if the surgery doesn't go well, Mom," he explained, "Jesus has a better place prepared for you."

His words were loving but unconvincing. I was in a panic. Maybe Ron Jr. was sure about all this, but I wasn't. I still didn't understand it at all.

FREE INDEED

As I was admitted into the hospital, panic turned to dread. I refused to go on with the surgery until a priest could be found to give me Communion. I didn't understand how Ronald Jr. and his friends could be so sure about God's presence. I was like a crazy person, wanting to take Communion like some people throw salt over their shoulder, "just in case." Unable to claim a personal faith of my own, I thought maybe "doing" Communion would be as acceptable to God as having a real belief in Him.

Minutes ticked away, but no one could find a priest.

Then, unexpectedly, a peaceful feeling came over me. Just before the surgery was to begin, I suddenly understood. God stepped in and rescued me. I was like a child too small to reach the light switch. Like a loving father, God saw His child stumbling around in the dark. He simply reached out over my head and quietly clicked on the light for me. Right there, on the gurney outside the operating room, I made a decision.

Journal Entry—January 4, 1972

How very strange that I could have received Jesus into my little heart so long ago and yet never really gotten to know who He is. But now, suddenly, in the twinkling of an eye, I know Him. Before, I accepted the fact that Jesus had died for mankind. Today, I realize He came and died for me.

Yesterday, I knew He was the savior. Today, He is my savior.

Yesterday, I understood that He is Lord of all the Earth. Today, I take Him as Lord of my little life.

I receive Him with open and such grateful arms; full of relief. I no longer want my life. I'm tired of it. I want His life. I can't make mine work, but for some strange reason, He wants to take it and try to make something of it.

In exchange for the mess my life has gotten to be, He has placed His peace in my heart; a peace I don't deserve and shouldn't have; nevertheless, it's mine! And it is the most wonderful

CHAPTER SIX

thing I have ever experienced. Like walking through a rose garden on a summer evening, the fragrance of it washes over my face and fills my lungs. I just lie here inhaling this peace, scarcely believing I'm in such a beautiful place.

I know He's here now. I know it. I don't hope it or wish it anymore. I know it as surely as I know my heart beats. I feel His hand in mine as surely as I feel this blanket around me. And now I know everything will be all right.

I will never want to belong to anyone else as much as I want to belong to Him, and I will never want to have anyone else be mine as much as I want Him to be mine.

I'm not afraid any more. I told the doctor we didn't have to wait for a priest any more. Jesus is in me now, deeper than even bread and wine can go.

He did not change the bread and wine for me today. He has come in person.

■ CHAPTER SEVEN

I don't even remember who brought a Bible to me after the surgery. But since I had to stay in the hospital for eleven days, I had a wonderful time getting to know this fantastic book. It had always been my habit to start at the beginning whenever I read any other book, so I did the same with this—I started with Genesis.

The Bible was more than a collection of words for me; it became my food. I feasted on those words with all the gusto of a starving person, and they buried themselves deep inside me. They filled a vast, lonely, empty hole in my heart that nothing had ever been able to fill before.

I read about a God who cherished me, who wanted to shelter and care for me. His Word spoke of a love and commitment so consuming that this God would fight for me and defend me. It described a love so strong that it would not settle for less than the best for me. God showed me that He was determined to correct and discipline me. He wanted to move me out of the way of life that was destroying me, and into a way of life that would cause me to prosper and be whole.

It wasn't long before I got to Leviticus 18:22-25. "You shall not lie with a male as with a woman; it is an abomination.... Do not defile yourselves with any of these things, for by all these the nations are defiled, which I am casting out before you. For the land is defiled; therefore I visit the punishment of its iniquity upon it, and the land vomits out its inhabitants." Soon after, I came to Leviticus 20:13. "If a man lies with a male as with a woman, both of them have committed an abomination."

These words took me completely by surprise. It was the first time in my life I had been confronted with the idea that God saw something wrong with homosexuality. It wasn't long before I read the New Testament. And by the time I got there, I wasn't surprised to find Romans 1:26-27 saying, "For this reason God gave them up to vile passions. For even their women exchanged the natural use for what is against nature. Likewise also the men, leaving the natural use of the woman, burned in their lust for one another, men with men committing what is shameful, and receiving in themselves the penalty of their error which was due."

You might think that in confronting this new information, I would have been offended or filled with dread. It was a brand new revelation to me, something I had never considered. But when I decided to accept it as truth from the lips of God, I began to understand why I so wanted to get out of my relationship with Marla.

Yet even with this new revelation, I would have to put my longing to be free of homosexuality on a kind of mental "shelf" for the time being. I may have wanted out, I may have agreed that God wanted me out, but there was no visible or imaginable way for me to get out.

Once home, I was under doctors' strict orders not to be sexually intimate for the next six weeks. I constantly sent up prayers of thanksgiving for those medical restrictions. I had so much to sort out.

I continued to pour myself into reading the Bible. I never realized how intriguing, and exciting, how interesting and clear it was. Why had I ever thought that I could never read and understand it by

CHAPTER SEVEN

myself? Later I learned that the Scripture itself says that it cannot be understood and interpreted by man's mind—only the Spirit of God knows the mind of God (1 Corinthians 2:11-16). However, when I received Jesus into my heart, I had received the mind of Christ. I was now able to understand the things of God because I had made a dwelling place for Him in my own heart.

I hid behind that Bible, trying to gain strength, searching for a way out of my intolerable lifestyle. Finally I had found some hope. It was like a light at the end of a long dark tunnel, but at times the light sure seemed to be an oncoming train.

I tried to tell Marla about my newfound love for Jesus, and I began sharing with her some of the things I was finding out about our relationship. To put it mildly, she was not pleased to hear any of it. Her threats turned into violent rages. Yet nothing she did stopped me. When my recuperation time was over, I returned to the prayer meetings with my son. Marla was not happy about it, but I went anyway and eventually switched to an adult meeting. I began going to these meetings with Jeanne Cook, an old friend from high school with whom I was getting reacquainted.

At the first adult prayer meeting I attended, the group began singing a song from Romans chapter 8. The tune was so pretty that I started to hum along. "Hmmm, hmmm, hmmm... 'In everything God works for good with those who love him.' Hmmm, hmmm, hmmm... 'If God is for us, who can be against us?' Hmmm, hmmm, hmmm." Then, without realizing it, I began to sing in a language I had never heard.

During the next meeting, as I was sitting peacefully in my chair, I began to realize I had something stirring inside me that needed to be said. But it was, again, in the language I didn't understand.

"Oh, no, God," I prayed silently. "You aren't going to get me to stand up and embarrass myself, are You? I don't even know what I'm doing yet. I'm too new at this. If You want me to deliver this, You are just going to have to kick me out of this chair." Suddenly, I was bolt upright and hearing myself speaking in tongues to the crowd of about two hundred people. To my great relief and delight, immediately someone stood up and gave the interpretation.

When the meeting was over, an Asian priest came over to me and began to engage in an animated discussion with me in Chinese. He finally realized, after I continued to stare at him blankly, that I had no idea what he was saying. "Where did you learn that language? That is an ancient Chinese dialect that very few people even understand today. And the person who stood up after you translated it perfectly!"

I was still standing there, mute with amazement, when Jeanne approached us.

"What happened to you, back there?" she asked. "It looked like someone physically kicked you out of your chair!"

I was beginning to understand what it meant to be baptized in the Holy Spirit. But Marla wasn't at all impressed when I tried to explain things to her. And I still saw no way to sever my ties with Marla. We had resumed our physical relationship because I saw no other way. But, mercifully, God sent me help again. I began to fall asleep during our times together.

What a crazy joke it was. Here was a woman who had never spent more than a couple of hours a night sleeping, and now I was falling asleep during a time when I had every reason to stay awake. Scripture says that "He gives His beloved sleep" (Psalm 127:2) and I guess that's what He started doing for me. I had so much peace inside that sleep suddenly began to overtake me.

It would, however, take another year of fear, threats and continuing abuse before finally I found the courage to reach out for help.

In the meantime, I was concerned about my husband. All our married life, he'd had painful mastoid infections. He had occasionally experienced dizzy spells, which somehow were related to the problem in his ears. Now, however, he was beginning to pass out entirely. It became clear something had to be done. By the time he finally went to see the doctor, the infection had wrapped itself around the nerves and muscles in his face. The doctor informed Ronald that either he had immediate surgery or he would be dead in six weeks.

CHAPTER SEVEN

After the successful surgery, I stood over Ronald in his hospital bed and began to realize just how much I needed, wanted and loved this man. It had been seven years since I had last told him, "I love you." Fear of Marla's threats had silenced me. Now, my heart was being prepared for change. God, through His gentle Spirit, began to woo me, to urge me back to my husband.

I learned something during that time. Cupid, the icon of Valentine's Day, has nothing on God the Father when He sets out to put two people together. No one has seen romance until they've watched God knit two hearts into one. For the past seven years, unknown to me, Ronald had begun his return to God, and he had been praying for our marriage. At the time, he was driving a delivery truck for a major bakery, and had a three-hour commute every day. He had been using the entire three hours to pray for us. He didn't know what was wrong, he didn't know what to do, but at long last he laid aside his "Father Knows Best" pride and turned to the real Father for answers.

Oh, so quietly and secretly, things began to change after Ronald's surgery.

For one thing, he began bringing me gifts. At first he wasn't especially romantic about it. He'd bring home from work a piece of jewelry or some small gift, and throw it to me across the living room with the casual comment, "I got this for you, by the way."

Then he started inviting me to join him at some of the union functions. And he returned from other meetings without going out with the guys afterward. He began holding my hand in public, and putting his arm around my shoulder when we were out together.

This was interesting, because ever since my trip to New York with Marla, she had been behaving just the opposite. She would not recognize our relationship in public. There was no holding hands, no expression of tenderness. Early in our relationship she had brought me little gifts, but those days were over.

As days passed, God began to change the people around me, even as He called me to change. Ronald was the one who paid attention to my needs. He was the one who began to show me that he cared. He showed me evidence of his love. Marla's possessive desperation stood out more and more conspicuously, and I was no longer interested in being someone's possession.

Not long after Ronald's surgery, he and I went away to a couples' resort in the Pocono Mountains. It was only the second time in our marriage that we had ever been away together without the children or friends. We stayed in a chalet with a heart-shaped bed, tub, and sink. Stately pine trees and the rolling Pennsylvania mountains surrounded the resort. Everything was beautiful, clean and romantic.

The more time Ronald and I spent alone, the more I knew that I was falling in love with him all over again. I also knew that I had to tell him that I loved him.

The Lord had to encourage me about it, however, because I was still very much afraid of Marla. God's Spirit whispered to me, "Tell Ronald that you love him. It will be okay. I will protect you. I will protect your heart."

"God," I responded, "I believe You will protect my heart, but You don't know Marla. She will kill me!"

"I am Lord of everything. Tell him."

There was no more thinking or choosing; I knew this was the time. So, for the first time in seven years, I told Ronald that I loved him. And what a celebration of love we had! Symphony! Trumpets! Cymbals! Fireworks!

That weekend with Ronald became all I had dreamed of during my New York weekend with Marla. We went home together, much happier than we'd been in years. And when Marla found out I was saying "I love you" to Ronald again, she was livid. Surprisingly, however, she kept her peace.

So many things happened that last year with Marla: my hysterectomy, receiving the Lord, being baptized in the Spirit, devouring the Scriptures, Ronald's surgery, falling in love again, saying "I love you" to my husband. They all were moving in one direction, leading me to a final conclusion. But one remaining event sent chills of urgency through me, bringing me to the end of myself.

CHAPTER SEVEN

"Ma! Ma!" Somewhere in the night, our nine-year-old daughter was screaming. Marie Anne had the covers over her head and her hands over her face when I arrived. I pulled away the blankets, but she would not take her hands away from her eyes. Try as I might, I could not get her to calm down. "They're coming at me!" she screamed. "The devil faces!"

Dear God, no! I thought. Had my daughter entered my old attic room? I slammed on the light switch and began to pray. I held her and prayed with her. "Honey, it will be all right. Jesus will protect you. He won't let you be hurt." I held her and rocked her and comforted her until she finally agreed to let me draw her hands away from her face. But her next words were like knives thrown straight into my heart.

"It's in your face! The devil face! It's in *your* face!" she shrieked.

She clutched at her face to cover her eyes again. I started praying, commanding the demons to leave. Then I began to praise the Lord and worship Him. I was still new at all of this, and I didn't know what to do for Marie Anne or for me, but I knew my Jesus now. I knew He would not let me down. I kept telling Marie Anne that God was there to help us. Gradually, she calmed down. The faces went away, and she was finally able to sleep.

The incident ended peacefully enough, but I knew what it meant. The relationship with Marla had to come to a final end. There must be no more delay. If I had to humble myself and tell someone what was going on in order to get some help, then so be it.

■ CHAPTER EIGHT

My friend, Jeanne Cook, was the only one I could imagine entrusting with my secret. I had grown up with her and now, without even thinking, I found myself running to her house. I was panicked, desperately in need of help.

I beat at her door and leaned against the doorbell until Jeanne came to answer. I don't remember exactly how I began, but I spilled everything out to her. I was so ashamed, and I expected her to be shocked and horrified. She listened patiently until I took a breath. Then, while I sobbed in her arms, she simply said, "That's no problem. Jesus can take care of that."

Her confidence was such a comfort, her acceptance such a relief. I knew I could trust her with anything. After we talked, Jeanne told me she knew a priest who was a counselor. I gave her permission to call him.

To my surprise, the priest not only came immediately, but he talked with me for two full hours. Finally, he told me that I had no choice. My very soul was at stake. I knew that I could lose everything—my marriage, my kids, my home. But I was no longer willing to live in hell, or to risk my soul. I would have to tell Marla to leave.

I had made a decision, and I would not turn back. But it had to be done quickly, while I still had the courage. I called Marla and asked her to come to the house. She sat down opposite me, but I remained standing. Without emotion, I told her I wanted her out.

"Excuse me? What do you mean, 'out'?"

I stood my ground. "'Out,' as in 'out the door,' 'out of my life,' 'leave and don't come back.' I don't ever want to see you again."

She tried to console me, then argue with me. When she knew that I was serious, she slumped onto the floor in a heap, sobbing. "Please don't send me away. We can just be friends. I'll be good."

Fortunately, the priest had warned me not to listen to any arguments or pay attention to any tears. I stood firm, like a robot without feeling, without emotion. I couldn't afford to feel sorry for her, or to regret what I was doing. If I did, all would be lost. I felt like I was watching the whole scene through another person's eyes. I couldn't believe that I was actually the one doing this.

In a remarkably short time, Marla gave up pleading and left. She attempted, in various ways, to get back into my life. She tried joining the prayer group that met at Jeanne's house, but Jeanne warned me whenever she was coming and I stayed home. Jeanne and her husband sincerely tried to minister to Marla, but soon she quit coming to their home.

I find it remarkable, in retrospect, that in a town the size of ours, she and I never crossed paths after that. I never saw her in the stores where I shopped. I never passed her in the streets. It was just as well with me. I didn't want to have to fight any more.

Sometime after my break with Marla, I was counseling with my prayer group leader, who asked why Ronald never came to church with me. I had told Ronald about being baptized in the Holy Spirit, but he had never been impressed about it. Try as I might, I could not convince him that he needed the new closeness to God that I had found. My prayer group leader responded with a question.

CHAPTER EIGHT

"What is it you're doing or not doing that is keeping Ronald from wanting to come back to church?"

Offended, I cried, "Me? But it's not me—it's him! I was the one who was hurt by the marriage, not Ronald!"

It took some honest prayer, but finally I heard the Lord say to my heart, "Forgive your mother-in-law."

Seven years before, we'd had a falling out. She had been offended by the actions of one of my children, and I had disagreed that punishment was necessary. We'd blown up at each other. She'd declared that she never wanted to see the child again, so I took my children with me and obliged her by storming out. Neither of us had been willing to reconcile. That was the last we'd seen of each other.

I sat down and began to write a letter asking for her forgiveness. It turned into a fourteen-page epic. On the advice of my group leader, I showed the letter to Ronald and asked if he thought it was appropriate. "Should I send it?" I asked him.

"Yes," he said quietly.

One week after I mailed the letter, I got a short note from my mother-in-law. She asked how the children were and told me that the weather was fine. I was disappointed that she mentioned nothing about my letter, but I let it go. At least she had accepted my apology.

A week later, as I was getting ready for the prayer meeting, I noticed that Ronald was getting dressed, too.

"Where are you going?" I asked.

"I'm going to the prayer meeting with you."

I was overjoyed until we got there. He sat in the back of the room, with his arms folded. He never sang or spoke, he just sat there. For three months, he sat in the same place, with the same closed expression on his face.

Then one night, he asked me to call Jeanne and Jim Cook to see if they were busy. "Why do you want to see them in the middle of the week?" I asked.

"I want them to pray over me for the baptism in the Holy Spirit," he explained.

FREE INDEED

My heart began to pound in anticipation. We went to their house and the three of us prayed over Ron as he knelt in their family room. It was wonderful. Within three months, Ronald and I were in leadership of the prayer group. Yet, I still hadn't confessed my lesbian past to him.

Even after the break-up with Marla, my sexual attraction for women did not change. For fifteen more years, I had to fight against those feelings. My good friend, Jeanne, was my only confidant during those years.

I threw myself into consuming my time with the Scriptures and godly activity. As long as I was reading the Word and involved in prayer ministry, I successfully fought off homosexual temptations. But sometimes things would get crazy, and I'd seem to be losing my grip. At these times, Jeanne was always there for me. She was the only one who knew about my struggle. I don't believe Jeanne ever realized the gift from God that she was to me during those years.

In response to my diligence to seek Him, the Lord began to take me on the most incredible therapeutic journey. So long ago, I had quit being a girl-child. Now, God began taking me back, helping me relearn and relive the childhood I had missed. With Jeanne, I began to talk out loud about my childhood for the first time.

When we weren't talking, I found myself studying Jeanne's every move. I studied how she dressed, how she walked, even how she put on make-up in the rearview mirror. She became my model of womanhood, and I copied her as a young girl imitates her mother. She began, in a sense, to re-mother me by giving me guidelines and boundaries, teaching me right from wrong, and disciplining me. She prayed with me and comforted me when I wanted to give up. She showed me the love of a genuine mother.

No one else had ever been a "real" mother to me. I had never learned what it was to be loved, nurtured and watched over. This friend from God was now pouring His love into that empty place that should have been filled by my mother. Jeanne comforted me when I was sad, she corrected and admonished me when I was out of order,

CHAPTER EIGHT

and she ministered forgiveness to me when I had done wrong. In her I found a person who constantly loved me unconditionally. She didn't pay attention to me because she wanted something from me. She paid attention because she cared about me. Her faithfulness gave me a visible picture of God's "motherly" concern for me.

Jeanne stuck by me during a horribly frustrating time, as I dealt with wave after wave of temptation, fantasy, guilt, loneliness, and disappointment. I struggled to stay clean, and I depended on her elbow in my ribs to bring me back to reality, whenever she noticed my eyes "wandering" toward other women. When pressures started to overwhelm me, we would go up to a cabin in the woods to pray and talk and dig and search for answers. In that secluded place, I had time to mourn over my lost childhood. I had time to get angry, and to get over my anger. Jeanne was the gentle "hammer" He used to keep pounding into my heart the idea that I was, indeed, loved and accepted.

In between the searching, we laughed and got silly. I was free to become an early adolescent at a slumber party, as we played music and danced. In these times, Jeanne was a real "girlfriend" to me. Jeanne would try to teach me all the different '50s dances from her childhood in Brooklyn, New York. Sometimes we were doubled over with laughter. We fixed each other's hair and played with make-up and laughed. That laughter was so sweet! There had been so little of it in my life.

In the evenings, it was great fun to sit in front of the fireplace and enjoy the times of quiet as Jeanne played the guitar and sang praises to God. It was my first real experience with a close—but healthy—female/female relationship. I was so thankful for friends, and for God's faithfulness! For the first time, I was comfortable being with another woman because we were alike. I had always felt like "one of the guys" with my brother and his friends many years ago. Now, at long last, I felt like "one of the girls."

■ CHAPTER NINE

Within the year that Marla and I broke up, I began experiencing numbness in different parts of my body. Then, one day, my right side collapsed. I thought I was having a stroke, and was immediately admitted to the hospital. For a week I underwent a battery of tests, but nothing conclusive was determined. Eventually the doctors told me that I had experienced a brain seizure. I was given medication to control seizures, then sent home.

Ronald and I prayed all the way home. We were convinced that I was dealing with something more serious than a seizure, so we asked God to show us if something more needed to be done. Within thirty minutes of walking in the front door, I collapsed again. This time I was not frightened. I knew that God was with me; I knew that I belonged to Him. Back in the hospital, more tests were given.

This time, the doctors found a tumor in my brain the size of a golf ball. I was told there was only a fifty-fifty chance of coming through the surgery alive; and even if I made it that far, they held out little hope that I could avoid having my right side paralyzed for the rest of my life.

FREE INDEED

We spent the next two months going through grueling preparatory tests. On December 9, 1974, I was admitted to the hospital for surgery, which was scheduled for four days later. Doctors told me that I'd be home by Christmas. Confidently, I had spent the previous two months getting all my shopping, gift-wrapping and decorating done, so that I would be ready for Christmas upon my return home.

I was very much at peace before the surgery. I knew, with Jesus, that I was in good hands. People from the prayer group called constantly to tell us they were praying. Ronald was there for me every step of the way. Waking up from the anesthetic, I remember thinking, at first, that I had died. All around me were bright lights and brilliant white surroundings. Then I realized I was in the hospital. I began to praise God that I had made it through alive, and began testing my arms and legs. Left arm, okay. Right arm, okay. Left leg, okay. Right leg... right leg. Right leg! *Oh well,* I thought, *what's one leg after all this.*

In the room with me was a young girl about thirteen years old who had been hit by a snowplow. She was in a coma and she moaned all day long. One of the nurses whispered to me, "She'll be a vegetable for the rest of her life." I remember praying for her, as I lay immobile on my bed, but I guess I must have been praying out loud all the time, without realizing it. After the girl went to a regular room, a nurse came and told me that she was getting better, and that now this nurse believed in the power of prayer. Wonderfully, the girl went home about two weeks before I did, her mind and body perfectly normal.

To my disappointment, I was not released from the hospital until New Year's Day. By this time I had lost the use of my entire right side and could not walk. The doctors didn't expect me to ever regain the use of my right side. They said I had too much brain damage and scar tissue to make that possible. "Physical therapy is pointless," they told me. Instead, I was sent me home with a walker. I don't think my doctors even expected me to use that walker, but they sent it with me anyway. Whatever small hope they may

CHAPTER NINE

have had that I would ever walk again, they had even less that I would ever get back the use of my right hand.

Doctors may have great expertise and knowledge, but fortunately they do not have the last word. Jesus has been given all authority and power both in heaven and on the earth, and He had determined a totally different prognosis for me. Getting there, however, was anything but easy.

Once I was home from the hospital, my life became a study in humiliation. I lost all semblance of pride; I couldn't even take care of my own most basic needs. Most degrading of all was the rented port-a-potty which we stored in the kitchen pantry, the only place accessible to me downstairs. I needed help with everything. Though I appreciated my friends coming over to pray and assist, it was terribly embarrassing to have them do all my housework. I had always been self-sufficient. In fact, the idea that I really could do it all myself was part of what had initially kept me from confiding in anyone. Self-sufficiency had helped keep all my secrets hidden.

Every morning, before Ronald left for work, he helped me get up and get dressed, then he carried me downstairs to the couch. There he tucked me in with a blanket so I could go back to sleep until the girls got up. By this time, Ronald Jr. was away in the military. Marie Anne and Sonjia, who were now teenagers, fed me breakfast and prepared a lunch for me to eat later.

During the day, the members of our prayer group stayed with me in shifts. No one wanted me to be alone in case I should have another seizure. Whenever they came over, those faithful people always prayed for me. A new shift would take over, and *they* would pray for me, too. I was prayed for in person several times a day, not to mention the countless other prayers which were offered up for me from a distance.

From the very start, I practiced using my right hand. It didn't work very well, but I insisted on trying. I resisted every suggestion to settle for being left-handed. I knew that if I compromised in that, I would never get back to normal. And I took up crocheting, of all things. Every day I struggled with the crochet hook. Most of the time, it took me all day just to finish one row. Now that I look back on it, it's amazing that I could do that delicate work at all.

Meal times were, far and away, the most comical times of the day. Twice a week, we continued our habit of having spaghetti. Having a not-too-tight grip on the fork with my right hand, and almost no control over its movement, I frequently slid my fork across the plate, and into the unsuspecting heel of my left hand which was gripping the plate for dear life. No one could ever be sure exactly on which side of the table my food would settle before my right hand would get the message to stop flying forward and head for my mouth. Fortunately, I learned to laugh along with the others as they witnessed my antics at the table.

I had to learn to walk without the benefit of feeling the floor with both feet. My left foot would move strongly and confidently forward, but then I'd have to pull my totally numb right foot across the floor to meet it. At first, all I could do was step, drag, step, drag. Eventually, I got the motion smoothed out, but quickly learned that slip-on shoes were a problem for me. Because I couldn't feel them on my right foot, slip-on shoes usually ended up on the floor far behind me, until some kind soul returned them.

Soon I gained enough confidence to leave behind the walker. Then I got rid of the cane. Finally, I walked on my own. It was a great day when I walked back into the doctor's office to show him what God had done for me. He was totally amazed, and had to admit that something had certainly happened to change my fate.

I was so proud to be able to walk again without anyone's help. Enough of my hair had grown back so that, although it was almost a crew cut, I stopped wearing a wig. One Sunday, when our family was asked to bring the gifts up to the altar at church, I insisted on helping. My right foot still had a tendency to turn inward when I walked, so I concentrated on keeping it pointed in what felt like a normal direction. I was so proud of myself until I went pack to the pew, and found my daughters giggling quietly, but uncontrollably. Evidently I had

CHAPTER NINE

over-compensated. When they regained their composure enough to talk to me, they informed me I had walked to the front "like a duck."

I worked hard, but never without the understanding that Jesus is the healer. Despite the doctor's hopeless prognosis, within three months, I regained the use of my right arm, hand and leg. Nevertheless, the road to normalcy was a long and hard one. My anti-seizure medication was so heavy that I was simply in a fog for much of the next three years.

■ CHAPTER TEN

By 1978, our youngest daughter was approaching her sixteenth birthday, and things had leveled out a bit. Ronald and I had been leaders in our prayer group for about four years. We decided to take a break from all the hustle and bustle by embarking on a camping trip through most of the major state parks across the country. Before we left, our priest recommended a Christian community in New Mexico as a stopping place. He thought they would allow us to park our camper for the night on their property.

When we arrived in Belen, New Mexico, and asked to stay the night, the community welcomed us. They even prepared rooms where we could sleep, which gave us a welcome relief from three weeks in a camper. While we visited, we had an opportunity to talk with the priest there about his vision for the community. The more we talked with him, the more we became convinced that God had a ministry for us in that state, too. Some day, we thought, we would move to New Mexico. We read Isaiah 40:3, and knew this Scripture was for us; that we, too, would be a "voice of one crying in the wilderness."

Back in New York, we excitedly shared our new vision with

our prayer group. Their response, though we assured them the call was still for the future, was to ask us to step down from leadership. Even if our move would be well in the future, they did not see how we could continue being committed to the group if we were being called elsewhere. This, of course, felt to me like rejection. It was understandable, but it still hurt.

The Lord released us to hand over the reins of leadership, and soon moved us to a nearby parish. Within two years we were asked to join the leadership at the new parish, even though they knew about the call to New Mexico still in our hearts.

This new move presented me with an interesting difficulty. From the ages of thirty-five to thirty-seven, I had been "flying high" with the Lord. Everything was new and exciting and I wanted to be part of it all. From the ages of thirty-seven to forty, I had essentially been anesthetized with drugs, so there was no opening for temptation. Now past forty, my medication had been reduced. My head was becoming clear enough to think deeply about things. Furthermore, we had moved into a condo that was far from my old prayer partners. My time was no longer loaded up with things to do. Being alone and not busy was so unfamiliar to me that I was afraid to face it. To take up my time, I began working at a nearby nursing home.

In 1979, five years after my first brain surgery and just as we were paying the last of my medical bills, I began to get sick again. I had only been working in the nursing home for about six weeks when, coming home one day, I became aware that something was very wrong. I recognized the old familiar symptoms of having a seizure. I went back to the doctor and was diagnosed with another tumor.

At first I was very angry with God. I had gone through this once, and by His grace, I had recovered. Why did I have to go through it all over again? Of course it did no good to ask questions; there was nothing I could do about it. But the seeds of anger and rebellion had been planted imperceptibly in my heart, ready to take root and sprout at the slightest opportunity.

This time, at least, I knew what to expect: tests, surgery, shaved

CHAPTER TEN

head, medicine, side effects. This tumor was much smaller, so my recovery was faster and easier.

I was in intensive care for a total of one and one-half days. I had surgery on a Monday afternoon and I was out of bed by that night. On Tuesday evening I requested the hospital dinner of corn beef and cabbage—I was ravenous! The nurses had not seen anyone eat so well and so soon after the heavy anesthesiology of brain surgery. They expected me to regret every bite of that cabbage, but I ate the whole meal and slept peacefully. By Wednesday morning, I was out of intensive care.

While I was in the hospital, God miraculously healed a young girl who was about ten or eleven years old. It was a similar incident to my first hospitalization. Her liver had been severed in an accident and the doctors did not expect her to live. I prayed with the girl and her mother that Jesus would come and heal her body. She was totally healed and went home from the hospital before I did. I was able to praise the Lord for His mighty healing power.

Nevertheless, I felt overwhelming guilt because I was sick again. We had just paid off the last of the hospital bills for the first surgery. I had been successful in keeping my lesbianism under control and our marriage was just coming back into romantic focus again. But now that would be affected by the increase in my medication. I was tired of having to fight the same battles over and over again.

Once I left the hospital, I went back to participating in prayer group again, and met a new member. Dan had just been released from six months in the hospital, recovering from a severe car accident which he had not been expected to survive. He had multiple fractures all over his body. I met him after he was all healed and put back together. Several people from the group had gone to the hospital to pray for him, and he subsequently became a member of our community. He and I instantly became friends.

Dan and I became a great emotional support for each other after I found out that he was struggling with homosexuality. We shared our deep secrets with each other without fear. We could understand one another's struggle. It was great to have a friend who understood. Dan was the only person besides Jeanne whom I had told about my lesbianism. Jeanne had always been there to listen, but she could never really identify with my feelings or understand my confusion in trying to deal with homosexual attractions.

About a year after this second surgery, my daughter Sonjia asked me to help her move to New Mexico. I planned to spend two weeks helping her settle into her new home, followed by two weeks visiting with my friend Sally, who had also recently moved to New Mexico. But soon after Sonjia and I had her things brought into her new house, we had a falling out. She was belligerent, letting me know that she didn't want my help. I figured that if she didn't want my help, I wasn't going to stay. I packed my clothes and hopped a bus to stay with Sally. Ronald wanted me to come home when I left Sonjia, but I refused. I wasn't ready to go home yet.

Before I'd received Jesus, I had let everyone else make decisions for me. I didn't realize I could make choices, and I never fought back. After each of the brain surgeries, I had spent time being a helpless invalid because of the medication. All my needs had to be met by others. Now that the medication had been reduced and its effects controlled, I began to assert myself and let out some of the "real" me. The change in my personality made it difficult for my family to live with me. They had a hard time accepting the fact that there was a capable and opinionated person emerging from inside me.

Something happened to me in the month that I spent with Sally in the desert. All activities stopped, and I began to spend a lot of time with the Lord. Each day Sally brewed some coffee in the morning, then headed off to work. I sat on her back patio, drank my coffee, and gazed toward the mountain fifty miles away. And I prayed for two or three hours at a time. Then I went swimming for the rest of the day. For a month, that's how I lived.

Until then, I had always feared being alone. During my childhood, Mother would leave for work in the morning, followed by my older sister. I was left alone to care for my brother and make sure both

CHAPTER TEN

of us made it to school. After school, when Charlie and I came home, the house was locked up and empty. We couldn't get in until either my mother or my sister came home from work. I remember winter days when my brother and I found a way to get into the garage so we could huddle there to keep from freezing until someone came home to let us in. Now, for the first time in my life, staring at that mountain and talking to God on Sally's back porch, I finally felt safe.

Nobody knew me there. I didn't have to talk about anything I didn't want to discuss. I didn't need to prove anything to anyone. I wasn't a wife. I wasn't anyone's mother. I wasn't anyone's familiar friend.

I had tried to be what I thought Marla wanted me to be. I had tried to be the wife I thought my husband wanted me to be. I was constantly trying to hide and bury the lesbian feelings to please God. And I was incredibly tired of trying to maintain it all. I made a decision in New Mexico that I was through pretending. I was going to be *me* whether anyone liked it or not.

I had always felt like a tomboy, so I bought myself a pair of jeans (men's jeans!) and a T-shirt. I cut my hair shorter, and just relaxed for four weeks. I kept my new look when I returned to New York. Jeanne met me at the train station and immediately noticed the change.

"What happened to you?"

"Nothing."

"Oh, no. Something happened to you. I didn't even recognize you."

"Well, what you see is what you get. If you don't like it, that's just too bad. This is who I am, and this is who I am from now on. If you don't like it, or anybody else doesn't like it, I don't care."

When I got home, I found out Ronald had rented our condo to tenants because we were having trouble maintaining it. This meant that we had to sell much of our furniture, pack most of the rest in storage, and move in with Jeanne and her husband. I was infuriated that this decision had been made without me. It wasn't that I objected to moving in with Jeanne, but it had all been decided for me. I deeply resented the implicit disrespect.

FREE INDEED

Jeanne's husband was never home and Jeanne was also working. Ronald had to do all the handyman stuff around the house. So that left me, as always, the one who had to keep house during the day. Housework again! It was a big split-level house with an eat-in kitchen, a den, a big family room, three bedrooms, two and one-half baths, and a huge living area. Between the four adults and Jeanne's three grown boys, there were piles of laundry. And, by default, all this had become my responsibility.

The seed of rebellion, born from anger, came out and asserted its right to be different. It came out most conspicuously in my wardrobe. When I had first accepted the Lord and had been baptized with the Holy Spirit, I wore only plain dresses. My only jewelry was a large crucifix, which I wore around my neck. This type of outfit, coupled with my lack of make-up, made me look like a nun. By the time my second brain surgery loomed near, I had begun to wear pants more often. They were women's pants, and I tried to be conscientious about wearing proper make-up, but something of my old disdain for being female was still reasserting itself. Now, however, the jeans I wore were men's jeans, the T-shirts were men's shirts, and my hair was cut like a man's.

I also began to realize, to my frustration, that the same old lesbian thoughts and desires were still in my head. I felt little interest in men, and continued to feel a sexual pull toward women—which made me angry. It was frustrating to constantly deal with the pressure of saying "no" to myself, constantly keeping my flesh under control. For years I had been struggling with unfulfilled desires. For years I had dealt with surgery and recovery. Was it never going to end? Was I going to be continually dealing with illness and fighting homosexual desires? How could anyone expect me to keep this up for a lifetime? How could God expect such superhuman strength? I never expressed it out loud to anyone, but inside I was almost ready to tear myself loose from this interminable self-control and self-denial.

■ CHAPTER ELEVEN

Even though I was tired of being "good," God did not stop His work. I had been trying to behave properly through will power alone, and I had come to the end of my strength. Now God began focusing my attention inwardly, on things I never suspected were related to my ongoing problem with lesbianism. As far as I understood, the only problem was indulging in the physical act. I did not understand that there was anything wrong on the inside. I assumed, now that God and I were working together, that I should just naturally want only those things that pleased Him. So I was frustrated and confused. Why would He let temptations keep coming to me, and then tell me in His Word that they were not good?

Strange as it may seem, I could not imagine that my past had anything to do with my ability to deal with the present. I didn't see that my way of thinking could actually cause bad things to happen to me—things that were not God's will for me.

I kept searching for healing. I went to every healing Mass, to every teaching on healing, even though I didn't really know from what I needed to be healed. The idea that lesbianism itself could be healed had never occurred to me. All I knew was that I had terrible pain inside, and I wanted the pain to stop.

In reality, I was still carrying around the weighty residue of childhood neglect and a history of unhealthy relationships. These ruled the way I reacted to events and to people's attempts to interact with me. My heart was loaded up with open unhealed wounds, tender to the touch, and it had become a reflex action to jerk myself back away from people for self-protection. I wanted closeness with people, but I dared not risk any further rejection.

Keeping my thoughts and feelings hidden caused people to misjudge who I was and what I really wanted or thought. They responded to the person I appeared to be and, of course, that never satisfied the real need in me. While I held people at a safe distance, the deep "me" cried out to be drawn close and embraced. I didn't see my own arms stretched out, pushing people away from me. I only saw the distance others kept from me and I translated that distance as, "they don't really know me, they don't really want me." It became a self-fulfilling prophecy. I refused to risk the pain of real heart intimacy, and guarded my heart from the very thing I so desperately wanted.

Often I sat down in self-pity to gaze on my sad, lonely estate. No one likes to face pain, to approach it on purpose and touch it. But wounds—whether physical or emotional—have to be cleaned out so they can heal, or they will fester. The poison from an old wound, having access to new and healthy tissue, has opportunity to create new infections, new problems, new pain.

Hebrews 12:12-13 says, "Therefore strengthen the hands which hang down, and the feeble knees, and make straight paths for your feet, so that what is lame may not be dislocated, but rather be healed." In other words, "Hitch up your pants, roll up your sleeves, and go fix what is broken before it is thrown out of joint altogether!" It was time to begin exposing the infection. It was time to apply proper salve, and to dress the wound with clean bandages so that I could really be healed.

CHAPTER ELEVEN

Two or three years after the brain surgery, I attended a retreat led by a Passionist priest and his female co-worker at a nearby monastery. I sat through all the talks, but I didn't understand what this man was saying; his vocabulary simply went over my head. Yet, somehow I knew he had a powerful message for me. Everyone else at the retreat raved about his messages, but I just smiled and nodded, saying nothing. I felt so stupid.

When I got home, Ronald asked me about the weekend. I tried to tell him what had happened, as best I could. After he listened to my feeble explanation, I added, "He is doing another retreat in a couple of weeks. Why don't you come with me, so you can tell me what he's talking about?"

Those retreats became a real turning point for me. They provided me with an understanding about my life's thought patterns. This priest focused on the fact that Jesus is right with us in the hardest of times, walking with us through those trails. Later, I began waiting before the Lord in silence, meditating on the Passion of Christ—His crucifixion. And the Lord began leading me back into my painful past, helping me discover wounds long buried under the anesthesia of "busyness." While holding His hand, I looked with Him at some things I had tried to forget. Together, we began forgiving people, readjusting old reactions, setting the crooked things straight again.

There was so much to forgive, and without forgiving, I knew I could never be healed. Unforgiveness is like a fingernail constantly picking a wound. Forgiveness allows a scab to form as the healing begins taking place.

During this time, I also learned to explore old memories through role-playing. I would tell Jeanne or someone else what I remembered, and why it hurt. With their help, I would re-enact the incident over and over, playing the roles of different people involved, trying to understand each person's involvement. Then I would go back in my memory with Jesus. As He held on to me, I would forgive each person who had hurt me. It was not easy. I was only able to do this with Jesus present to help me. But eventually, wound after wound was healed, as forgiveness allowed me to let go of hurts and bitterness and pain.

Ronald and I continued working with the Passionist priest for five years, helping with retreats as we grew in our own understanding. In the process of participating in these workshops and support groups, my confused mind was beginning to make some sense. I started having dreams that were revealing and healing.

Father John taught me to look inside myself. I learned to look at my childishness. I learned how to be myself—to discover who I really am and how to make my own choices, rather than trying to be a reflection of the people around me. I began to dialogue with myself, constructing a bridge between my head and my heart. I started to look at the root causes for some of my problems. At last I told Father John about being a lesbian. Now, three people knew—but none of them was my husband.

This enormous commitment to healing did not provide a quick fix. Countless memories of childhood were brought up to the surface of my consciousness, recreating pain and anger as I considered them afresh. Memories of past abuses were added to the fresh indignities of present rejections: the prayer group's rejection of our leadership, the rejection of my input in the decision to rent the condo and move, Sonjia's rejection of my good intentions to help her. My heart was screaming out, "It's still here! It's still happening to me!"

During the day, I was able to keep my feelings at bay. But they came out after dark to play with my head. Worn out from the day's activities, I would wake up in the middle of the night feeling restless. I turned on the television and filled my sleepy head with R-rated movies, viewing things at night that I would never let anyone catch me watching in the light of day.

Under the veiled excuse of "relaxation," I fed the very thing in me that God wanted me to kill. The late-night airwaves are filled with sexual innuendoes and fantasies. Every wicked thing people

CHAPTER ELEVEN

would never do in public is satisfied vicariously on TV. By watching, I nurtured and built up in the darkness the very thing I was trying to tear down in the day.

I didn't realize it, but I was actually preparing myself for a fall. I was building a road down which Satan would easily lead me. I was giving aid and comfort to my own enemy.

Journal Entry—July 5, 1982

The week that I have been home from the retreat has been awful. My first day home, Ronald and I had a big fight over Marie Anne. Then he and I began going round and round about the car situation. He still doesn't see that there is any need to have a car available to me during the day.

On Tuesday, the day after I got home, at 8 PM, I got a call from Mom that Uncle David had died that evening. I was devastated. I cried for a long time—alone in my room—before Ronald came to tell me to take it easy and stop crying. I complained that he always seemed to be there for everyone else, but not for me. He denied that was so, and I cried some more.

Going to the wake on Wednesday night was awful. Since the Lord unbound my heart, things have been very painful.

When I got to the funeral home and walked up to the casket, the tears began to roll down my face. Then I saw my aunts standing nearby. I thought my heart would break. We hugged and cried. Then Ronald and I knelt down to say a prayer. I could not believe Uncle David was dead.

He looked so alive lying there, better than when I had last seen him. I could not hold back the tears and sobs.

Ronald was very annoyed. I only stayed in the visitation room a few minutes and I had to leave. Now I was crying uncontrollably out in the hall. My brother-in-law came and put his arms around me to console me. The next thing I knew, my father was there, asking me if I was all right. He walked with me for a minute, until I calmed down. Then we went back inside. I don't think Ronald even knew I was gone.

I would not have thought about going back a second night, except that I knew I had to go back for my own sake. The second night was a little better. I had prayed that day for acceptance and it came. God was good to me.

When I looked at my Uncle David, there were tears, but I did not see my uncle. I saw a shell and I knew that he was with the Lord. All I could think about was how grateful I was that I had had an opportunity to pray with him such a short time before this, as he asked Jesus into his heart. At least I knew that Uncle David would be with me again, when I went home with the Lord.

■ CHAPTER TWELVE

One night I dreamed about visiting a convent. There were many floors, rooms, and stairways. There were also many nuns, some wearing habits and some in street clothes. I had been assigned a room for my visit, but every time I left that room, I got lost. I went up and down staircases; one of the nuns saw me and said I did not belong in that part of the building. She gave me directions, but when I tried to follow them, I got lost all over again.

One nun, more than any of the others, tried to help me find my way. She must have had cancer or a similar disease; one side of her face seemed to be missing her jawbone. But, even though her face was deformed, she had a beautiful spirit. I did not know any of the other nuns, but this one I always trusted.

At one point in the dream, someone showed me a person who looked like the Pope. He had white doves, their wings spread, perched on his outstretched hands.

The nun said that I should go up the stairs to the place where he was standing. On the way up, there were many rooms with open doors to many temptations. I kept taking my eyes off the Pope to glance through each door, to see what was going on in each room. But every time I took my eyes off the Pope and his doves, I lost track of him.

Again I was lost.

I didn't understand this dream at first, but the danger of peeking into temptation's doors was about to be revealed to me. No one can flirt with temptation and not be seduced by it. I was about to learn a devastating lesson the hard way.

At one of the early retreats, I had met a woman named Tina. Quickly we became fast friends, even though she was much younger than me. Tina was a very needy person with a lot of pain and abuse in her own life. There was a spiritual "recognition" there; we understood each other's pain. At first we talked for hours. She cried and I comforted her. Soon the comforting turned into long hours of counsel and prayer. I knew I was getting too emotionally involved, but I thought, *I have it all together. I can handle this.* After all, I had been "handling" things very well for many years. I didn't have any insights into my own feelings but, by this time, I had vast experience in keeping everything under control.

In me, Tina had the mother figure she'd been missing. And I was glad to provide the nurturing she needed. I knew how to do it right for her. So I tried ignoring my growing attraction to her. I figured I would always have these desires, so I'd better learn how to control them.

I decided to test my self-control by going off with Tina for a whole weekend. Could I maintain control even under such strong pressure to give in? The end of the weekend revealed a disappointed Tina, but a very satisfied Barbara. I had kept control of myself. I had not fallen into sin. I was strong. I could have an emotional relationship with her without actually falling into sexual sin.

But it wasn't long before we began to develop the same jealousy that had existed between Marla and me. The relationship was kind and non-abusive, but something was still wrong. We became increasingly concerned about the other person's activities and

CHAPTER TWELVE

friendships. More and more we became one another's sole preoccupation. We didn't want to do anything without the other. I still loved and respected Ronald, but I was obsessed with Tina.

After three years of keeping our cool, Tina and I finally became physically involved. It was sweet and terrible at the same time. I cared deeply for this broken person. But suddenly I found myself caught up in the old lie of a double life.

On the one hand, I was a wife who openly loved her husband and family, but who kept a dark secret from them. On the other hand, I was a lesbian lover who cared deeply for another woman, but hid that relationship. I became panic-stricken; I had to get out. I wasn't ready to reveal my past secrets, and I certainly couldn't handle a collection of new ones. *God, how could this have happened again?* I wondered over and over. *I thought this was all over, finished, taken care of!*

The Lord let me know, in no uncertain terms, that I had to stop this behavior. This time, it was so much harder. I cared deeply for Tina, even though I knew it was wrong. I loved her, even though it was a sinful form of love.

But the Lord was unrelenting, and I knew better than to disobey Him. I was afraid that when I confronted Tina, I wouldn't be able to go through with it. So I brought help. I went to see her with a Bible in one hand and a crucifix in the other. I sat across from her in a restaurant holding these two things like shields in front of me as I talked to her. We cried a lot and made a pact that we would just be friends from that day on. But I knew that we would not be able to spend long hours talking ever again.

I was broken and crushed, because I had so stupidly given Satan the power to ruin a beautiful friendship. I was weighed down by guilt and shame for pulling another Christian down with me into sin. It took many years to work through the hurt and humiliation. And long after reconciling myself with my own failure, I found that, as usual, I had not been the first woman for Tina. There had been others. It took even more time to get over the realization that

I had been deceived by someone who seemed trustworthy. Could I ever trust a woman again?

Father John was beginning to pester me about revealing my lesbian struggles to Ronald. I was sure neither of us could deal with that. So, a short time later, I made up an excuse to convince Ronald that we should quit going to the Passionist retreats.

At last, in 1986, we relocated to New Mexico, moving into a small prayer community south of Albuquerque. We spent the next six months in prayer and contemplation. We were out in the desert and I was at peace again, spending hours in prayer, gazing at the same mountain I had enjoyed on my earlier visit.

There seemed to be no temptations here, no distracting activities. I had time to reconnect with my son and daughters who were all in New Mexico by this time. I could bond again with my grandchildren. I had always found myself running from retreat to prayer group to convention, looking for healing, looking for people who understood healing. I had never defined in my head what I needed healed. I simply knew that there was a lot of pain still inside me, and that I wanted it to stop.

Journal Entry—January 31, 1983

The dream starts out in a hospital room. I am a nurse, taking care of a dying woman. She has a strange disease that has made her shrink and shrivel up. She is very ugly and only about the size of a medium-sized baby doll. She keeps writhing in pain and asking for help. She also keeps asking me to cover her ugly head.

At one point, Marie Anne comes in the room and I tell her not to look, but she does. She is sick at the sight. I ask Marie Anne to go to the hospital nursery and get me a receiving blanket, because this woman needs to be wrapped up. Somehow, I get a hold of an experimental drug. I figure, "What can it hurt to try? She is dying anyway. Maybe it will help her to live." I give her the injection.

CHAPTER TWELVE

Next, I am talking to some other nurses. And then I must go back to my patient. When I return, I see she has greatly improved. She wants food and drink, so I hurry to get it for her. When I return and feed her, she expands and fills out until she becomes totally normal-sized and well.

We dance and hug and rejoice, because the Lord has performed a miracle. We ask all the other nurses and doctors to come and see. Many come in and look, but they do not seem to be much affected. I find myself very much in love with my patient, who has not only become well, but is very beautiful and feminine.

All of a sudden, I am so happy and overjoyed that my patient is well, and we embrace. We embrace so closely, in fact, that I actually merge into the now-beautiful healed woman.

■ PART THREE

Restoring What the Locust Had Eaten

■ CHAPTER THIRTEEN

In the New Mexico desert, I thought I was finished with all the intense work of self-examination. So I was totally surprised by God's next step for me. It wasn't a step I knew how to request. It was, instead, a gift God wanted to give me.

One day Ronald, my friend Sally and I were driving through the Jemez Mountains. The drive was nothing new; we had done this many times before. It was fall. There was some snow on the ground, and fresh snow was beginning to fall, but we were on well-traveled roads. I knew from experience that there was no danger of getting stranded here. The roadways were so warm that snow melted on them.

So why, I wondered, did I feel a rising panic in my chest?

I looked cautiously out the window again. The snowflakes were growing larger and fatter, until they no longer fell. They began to float, slowly drifting left and right, settling to the ground only after a long meandering trip through the air.

I was terrified of these floating giants, but I had no idea why. They filled the air, draping over the car like a white shroud. It was as if someone had taken a feather pillow and ripped it open over the car.

FREE INDEED

The feathers kept drifting aimlessly and ominously all around me.

And what was my response? I lay flat on the floor of the van, seized with terror, shaking uncontrollably. Ron and Sally had no idea what to do with me.

Finally, the snow stopped falling, and as quickly as it had started, the panic stopped. Sally informed me that we were going to do some serious praying about my strange, mindless fear. Within a few days, she and I checked ourselves into a local motel for the specific purpose of spending as much uninterrupted time together as we could, seeking the Lord's counsel.

We had hardly begun, when my belly was seized with a violent gripping pain, as though someone had caught my bowels in a huge and powerful vice. Immediately we went into prayer and within a short time, Sally saw something in her spirit: a pitiful, frightened, three-year-old girl standing in the midst of a cloud of white feathers. A white rooster landed at her feet with a thud, then staggered around as if it were drunk. A man with a baseball bat stood in front of the little girl.

Suddenly, I remembered it all. Of course, I was that little girl. We were in my grandfather's yard, and my uncle had just hit his prize rooster. Uncle David had scooped me up in my panic and had taken me down into a cellar, where he had molested me. As he brought me back upstairs, he made very sure no one was watching. Then he looked me in the eye and told me not to tell anyone what had happened, not to even remember it. Sally and I both realized that the fluffy white snowflakes had triggered the memory of those floating white feathers. Subconsciously, I had relived the terror of a three-year-old being handled so obscenely.

This event had happened before my mother had even started taking me into her bed, so it had served to prepare the way for even worse things. From both these abuses, I learned to simply shove painful, disagreeable thoughts about the past down deep enough into my mind so that they wouldn't continue to hurt. I could either bury them and survive, or feel them and die.

CHAPTER THIRTEEN

Now I understood why my Uncle David had asked forgiveness of me on his deathbed, when I'd prayed with him to receive Jesus. I had given it freely, not knowing why he wanted forgiveness. I hadn't been ready to face the past incident when my uncle asked for forgiveness, but God knew I would freely give it when the time was right. God is always thinking ahead. How else could He have brought me to this profound experience?

During the next twenty-four hours, I wailed and sobbed. I cried and prayed, as God expelled from me all the demons that had gained access to my heart, controlling and distorting my thinking and emotions. I didn't know, at the time, that God was dealing with evil spirits. I only knew that it was the most intense and wrenching time of prayer I had ever experienced. I'd sleep fitfully for a few minutes, gathering strength for the next round of warfare for the freedom of my soul. I was not controlling things. God gave me rest periods, but He was quickly back at work, exorcising the evil from my mind, my heart and my body.

Morning broke at last, and the battle seemed to be over. We still didn't know what all the anguish had been about, but I was soon to find out. Worn out from exhausting prayer, my friend and I went to the mall to clear our minds; there was nothing like a little "people watching" and window-shopping to relax. As we sat quietly on a bench, Sally gently elbowed me.

"Barbara," she said, "you are staring at something. What are you looking at?"

I suddenly realized, in utter surprise, that for the first time in my life, for the *very* first time, I was checking out men! Never in my life had I ever watched men walk by me—never! In the past, I had always concentrated my energies on *not* scoping out the women in the vicinity.

Oh, no! I thought. *Out of the frying pan and into the fire! Now I have to watch myself in the opposite direction.* I laughed out loud at my latest "problem," realizing that this was what women are supposed to feel. Finally, at fifty-one years of age, I was discovering what it felt like to be female. Like the patient in my dream, I had gone through a miraculous procedure and found myself becoming whole, healed, and female.

What a long road it had been, filled with delays and dangers before finding victory. It was similar, I thought, to the pioneers' frustrations and final relief in crossing the repetitive and seemingly endless slopes of the Rocky Mountains. I had always struggled and labored to get up each mountain. Then, flushed with the victory over one obstacle, my joy would be dashed as another mountain immediately loomed before me. No matter how many mountains I successfully crossed, there always seemed to be a new one just ahead. There was no time to rejoice in one victory; another challenge had to be immediately engaged.

Now, cresting this new mountain, the most awesome spectacle splashed against my eyes. I had come, in my spirit, into what seemed like the open expanse of an endless meadow. The mountain fog lifted and I was dazzled by a full spectrum of colors. The grass was greener; the sky was bluer. I was stunned to see what the world really looked like.

I was feeling such freedom and relief because the battle of my mind seemed finally over. Sally hardly gave me time to enjoy my liberation, however; she started pushing me to tell Ronald all about my past and about what had recently happened. I adamantly refused. All I wanted now was to live like a normal wife and mother. Why risk losing everything? "For what?" I protested. "For the pleasure of someone else knowing what a messed-up life I've led?" I had made it through all this and had managed to keep my marriage intact. Why should I risk destroying my relationship with Ronald just to confess something out loud?

Finally, overcome with dread, I went to my room and cried out to the Lord. My worst fear, that He was the one who wanted me to tell Ronald, was starting to seem like reality. Needless to say, I was horrified by the idea.

I wept. I wrestled. I shouted, "Why, God? Why? Why? Now

CHAPTER THIRTEEN

that I finally have freedom, is it to be taken away from me? Is this the price I will just have to pay for the lifestyle that I lived?"

As it turned out, I had run out of time for making my own decision. God had decided for me.

Journal Entry—November 23, 1988

Today, I told Ronald about my past. That sounds like it was easy, but it was one of the hardest—no, the hardest thing I have ever had to do. The brain surgery was easier.

Ronald found me sitting and looking out the window towards the mountains. I was crying and sobbing. I knew the Lord was asking me to reveal my past to Ronald, but before I felt I was ready to begin, Ronald walked in on me.

I tried to brush him off when he asked me what was wrong. But I hadn't had time to wipe the tears away, and I was obviously a wreck, so Ronald wouldn't take "nothing" as an acceptable answer. When he pressed for an answer, I just cried all the louder.

"Come on, now. How bad can it be?"

I said, "It's not about now, but it's about the past."

"How bad can it be? Did you have an affair or something?"

"No, it's worse than that!" I cried hysterically.

"Tell me what's wrong! I want to know."

"Okay. It's about Marla. She and I... I was a lesbian, but... it's hard to talk about it... please forgive me! Please don't leave me!"

The next moment was the most incredible of all my life. I saw Ronald stand before me and spread his arms out from side to side, beckoning me. "I forgive you. It's in the past. I love you very much."

I was in his arms before I remember getting up, and there I stayed. Together we cried and cried and cried.

When we could talk again, we began to share with each other as we had never shared before. I told him about my uncle and what had happened. I told him about the healing that the Lord had done in the Jemez Mountains. For the first time, I was able to rejoice with Ronald over the miracle that had happened, about being free at last. I never realized how much I needed to share my victories with Ronald.

Ronald wanted to know everything. No more secrets! He wanted to know so that he would never do anything that would remind me of the past, nor hurt me in any way.

The freedom to tell Ronald everything was matched only by the freedom I experienced when God delivered me in the mountains.

■ CHAPTER FOURTEEN

As soon as I told Ronald about my healing, he began urging me to tell the children. "Not only that," he insisted, "but after we tell the kids, we were going back to New York and tell our friends there, and then we were going to tell the world!"

My response was definite and immediate: "No!"

My relationship with my kids had just been healed and re-established. Why should I risk the loss of their respect? All I wanted was to live like a normal wife, mother, woman.

"But how can you *not* tell people that you're healed?" Ronald insisted.

"Easy. I don't want to do it."

Ronald pressed on. "There are people out there who are hurting, just the way you were hurting all those years. How can you not tell them there is healing and hope?"

"Why should I tell anyone? No one else knows that I was anything but me. I'll tell Jeanne, because she knows a lot about my past, and she deserves to know. Nobody else needs to know that I was anything but a wife and mother. Stirring all that up would be stupid!"

FREE INDEED

But Ronald was insistent—and patient. "It would be the end to all the secrets," he explained.

In the end, I had to agree with him. No one should have to go through that kind of pain alone, as I had done for so long. I came to see that it was my responsibility to let people know that there *is* a way out; that there *is* hope and healing for women and men caught in homosexual behavior.

Within a few months, we told the children what had happened to me, and explained to them our plan to go public with the story. The first one we told was Marie Anne.

"What is the matter?" she asked when we invited her over to talk. "It sounds serious."

"You're right. It is."

As soon as we were sitting down together, Marie Anne asked, "Are you and Dad getting a divorce?"

"No," I explained. "It's not about the present—it's about the past."

After she heard the story, Marie Anne's first comment was, "You cheated on my father! How could you cheat on my father?" Before I could respond, she added, "And you never wanted to have me in the first place. 'Auntie' Marla told me you didn't want me. She told me that when I was about eight years old."

I was flabbergasted! I had no idea that poor Marie Anne had been living under such a cruel misconception.

"When I got pregnant with you, it was not good timing," I explained. "Lots of things were going on, but they had nothing to do with you. I was worried because of all that I had gone through during the pregnancy. After all the drugs I had been taking and all the emotional turmoil, I was afraid that you wouldn't be normal. I was so grateful that you were okay. You were a gift from God. He used you to cement your father and me together. Once you were born, I spoiled you rotten. I loved you so much. It's not true that I didn't want you! I was just afraid for you."

When I told our daughter Sonjia, all she said was, "Well, that

CHAPTER FOURTEEN

sure brings a lot of pieces together, and makes sense out of some things." She started listing things that she had never been able to explain. "I always thought it was Dad having an affair with 'Auntie.' I just couldn't figure out how he could do that. I wondered why she was always there. I couldn't figure out why Dad put up with that, unless he was having an affair with her."

Ron Jr. was the only one who was really emotional about the revelation. It came at a very bad time for him. I kept asking him to forgive me, because I knew that he was the one who had suffered the most. He was the oldest, and saw more than any of the others—more than he had wanted to see. I remembered when I had told him that "Auntie" was leaving for good, all those years ago, he had said, "It's about time." He had been hurt more by my sin than either of the other two children.

When I left his house that day, he seemed to be at peace with everything. But two days later, I got a phone call from him. "I've thought about what you said, and I don't agree with the idea of going public. It's okay, and it's all in the past, but I don't want other people to know."

"Ron, I wasn't asking your permission," I responded. "I'm sorry that you don't approve. But I can't just sit here in silence while there are people who need to hear. I'm just letting you know what we're getting ready to do."

A while later, I got a scathing letter from Ronald Jr. and his wife, describing how they thought I needed psychiatric help. I was going to ruin their lives. What would happen to them once this came out in public? It could ruin their careers! At the end of the letter was Ronald Jr.'s signature.

With that, I was exiled from my son's life. I was not allowed to have any contact with Ronald Jr. or his children for five long, lonely years. To this day, I don't really remember all that was in that letter. It was so disturbing that I had to ask the Lord what to do with it. Finally, after I prayed over it, I lit a match and burned the letter to ashes. I had to give my son and the whole situation over to the Lord.

105

FREE INDEED

For five years, I mailed our Christmas and birthday presents to Ron Jr.'s family. For five years, I mailed the Christmas presents that arrived from my parents for their great-grandchildren. Day after day, I craned my neck as I drove around town, trying to catch an occasional glimpse of my grandchildren walking to school. Ronald talked to Ron Jr. on the phone just once during that time. Our son could not understand how his father could have forgiven me for what I had done.

The first step of telling the children was accomplished. Now Ronald decided that it was time for us to go back to New York and tell our friends there.

The first person we went to see in New York was Dan. As soon as we began to share what the Lord had done for me, Dan covered his ears. "Don't tell me. I don't want to know!"

Dan knew that if he heard healing from homosexuality was possible, he'd have to do something about it, and he couldn't handle the thought of having to change. "I don't want to hear what you have to say! I'm very happy the way I am! Don't tell me."

But it was too late. He *had* heard, and Dan's love for the Lord and the compassion of Jesus' Spirit working within him would not let him keep his hands over his ears for long.

Dan began his own journey down the same road I had traveled. Once we began working with people in Albuquerque, he participated in our twenty-week program through long-distance phone calls. Every time we found more books and counseling resources, we sent them to him.

Our next stop was telling our closest friends in the old prayer group. Many were greatly shocked and offended even to talk about such a subject. They seemed to feel betrayed that I had kept such a secret from them. My healing messed up all their settled opinions about being gay.

Many of our friends had family and friends involved in homosexual behavior. These Christians had given up believing change was possible for their gay friends, and had stopped talking to them

CHAPTER FOURTEEN

about it. Most of them had come to believe that homosexual behavior is caused by a genetic condition, which cannot be helped. It was less stressful to accept as fact that God made some people gay. It is so much easier to accept something as God's will, than to remain in a seemingly endless battle for healing and health.

■ CHAPTER FIFTEEN

In 1989, when I was fifty-two years old, I read a newspaper article about Exodus International, the largest ex-gay ministry in the world. The article explained the types of ministry available, and it shared some testimonies of people who had been set free from homosexuality. So there were others like me? How I ached to meet them! The article mentioned that the annual Exodus conference would occur soon. People from all over the country were meeting together to share, to learn, and to worship the Lord. I made up my mind to go.

As I made preparations for the trip, I had a dream one night. In my dream, I saw picketers in front of the University of New Mexico with signs saying, "I used to be, but I'm not any more."

A few days later, I arrived at the conference. To my amazement, person after person passed me wearing T-shirts that said, "I used to be, but I'm not any more. 1 Cor. 9:6-11." Without a doubt, I had come to the right place!

Suddenly, after feeling so alone and unusual, I was surrounded with people who were in the process of leaving homosexuality.

FREE INDEED

They were in various stages along the way, from the person who had just begun the journey, to people who had been walking in freedom for many years. Each person's face reflected joy, expectation, and satisfaction.

The first evening, we had a special service just to praise and worship Jesus before we began our week of workshops. As our voices began to rise in that assembly hall, I looked around me. There were men and women everywhere, lifting up their hands, reaching out for their Savior, their champion. They were dancing for joy, kicking up their heels, shouting in celebration; they were on their knees, on their faces, unashamedly weeping in gratitude, pouring out their love for Him with all of their hearts, with all of their might, with all of their energy.

The Bible says, "to whom little is forgiven, the same loves little" (Luke 7:47). All I could think of was the sinful woman at Simon's house, washing Jesus' feet with her tears, wiping them with her hair. These men and women were washing His feet with their tears, so great was their gratitude, so immense was their love for the Lord.

And the sound of it! This group of three hundred was mostly men, and their voices carried a depth and a passion that resonated like French horns and the blast of trumpets. The air trembled with joy.

The next day, I found out that Exodus, at that time, had been around for thirteen years. All at once I got angry. Why was it that I had never heard of Exodus until now? Why had it been such a secret? Why, when I so desperately needed help, didn't I know that Exodus existed? If only someone had told me, I wouldn't have gone through everything alone. I could have had help and company and support.

In that instant, I realized that Ronald was right. I couldn't keep silent. I was not that unusual. I needed to be the voice of at least one person crying out in the wilderness, "You *aren't* alone. There *are* people who have been down this road before, who know how to help and who are willing to stand by you. There is hope to escape this lifestyle!"

CHAPTER FIFTEEN

Back in Albuquerque, I began to prepare for my first public testimony. We were involved with a large interdenominational prayer group called God's People of Praise Community. Naturally, I was concerned about the reaction of our church friends. These people only knew me as a nondescript wife, mother, and grandmother. I had not yet been there long enough to know anyone very well, nor had I been deeply involved in any of the group's ministries.

In my darkest moments, I could envision my revelation destroying any chances I might have developed to establish close friendships. My "ministerial" career would be over before it had even begun. Oh well, it was all scheduled now, and there was nothing to be done but try and get some notes together that would put everything into some kind of chronological order. One of the things that Ronald and I disagreed about was whether or not he should be there with me. When we got to God's People of Praise and talked with leadership, they insisted that Ronald should stand with me.

I was nervous. I had always been a poor oral reader, and it didn't get any better when I stood in front of people. Ronald finally had to help me read the scriptures. When he got to Isaiah 40:3, Ronald began to weep: "The voice of one crying in the wilderness: 'Prepare the way of the LORD; make straight in the desert a highway for our God.'"

I also used 1 Corinthians 6:9-10 in my testimony, which says, "Do you not know that the unrighteous will not inherit the kingdom of God? Do not be deceived. Neither fornicators, nor idolaters, nor adulterers, nor homosexuals... will inherit the kingdom of God."

Afterwards, a woman named Dorothy asked to speak to me. "As you began to read the scripture from First Corinthians, I couldn't figure out which of those things you could have done. I kept wondering, *What did this woman do, murder babies?* When you said you got out of the lesbian lifestyle, I almost fell over. I had no idea there was healing for homosexuality."

Later on, Ron and I began to see Dorothy on a regular basis to help her deal with issues in her own life that had led her into struggles with lesbianism.

FREE INDEED

The church was abuzz for a week with the subject. Many people were moved to tears because Ronald stood up there with his arm around me as I spoke. The power of God to restore my life and save my marriage gave many hope for their own marriages. Maybe they weren't struggling with secret homosexuality, but they had plenty of other problems.

I was more nervous the next time I spoke, because my second testimony was to be given during a mixed service, including both men and women together. Since then, it has not been hard at all for me to get up and speak. God has enabled me to do something that I never would have thought I could do. Now I can talk to groups calmly and with assurance, even without notes. All I do is share the love and mercy that God has shared with me.

Before I gave my testimony, Ronald and I talked with the leadership at God's People of Praise, to let them know that we were available to minister to anyone who was seeking freedom from homosexuality. Someone had just come to them looking for help. The week before I gave my testimony, we went to talk with this person and God worked freedom for him, too.

About six months later, we started a regular support group. Now we pray and counsel with people, both in person and over the phone, who are involved in homosexual behavior, as well as with those who struggle to resist homosexual temptations, or who have family members in trouble. We decided to call our outreach "Free Indeed Ministries," because my favorite Scripture, the one that most describes my life and my resurrection, comes from John 8:34-36,

"Jesus answered them, 'Most assuredly, I say to you, whoever commits sin is a slave of sin. And a slave does not abide in the house forever, but a son abides forever. Therefore, if the Son makes you free, you shall be free indeed.'"

■ CHAPTER SIXTEEN

Ronald Jr. returned to my life as suddenly as he had turned away. Five years after our last conversation, he called Marie Anne and asked if she thought we would receive a call from him. Soon after she reassured him, he called Ronald Sr. Within days, he phoned again to ask me about getting together for lunch.

I tried to maintain my composure as I told him I would be glad to see him. When we met, we began a conversation as though we had never been apart, as though we simply picked up in mid-sentence from five years ago. We never talked about why he left, or about anything emotional. He never mentioned my past or my going public and starting the ministry. It just wasn't important anymore.

God's grace had reunited us. But, following close on the heels of that euphoric moment, three of my life's most painful years began.

During a prayer meeting at God's People of Praise in 1992, something said by the speaker triggered a rush of memories in me. Up to this time, I had remembered only fragments of what happened in my mother's bedroom. These memories had always been like tiny pieces of a puzzle, occasionally dropping onto the table of my memory. Now and then all the edge pieces seemed like they were joining up and displaying themselves before me, but I was always able to quickly sweep the arm of forgetfulness across that table, wiping them back into the box. Another time, it would be a few corner pieces assembling themselves in front of my eyes, but again, I wiped them away.

This time, though, it was as if someone stood over the table, poured out all the pieces at once, and they fell perfectly into place. Before I could brush them aside, they formed the whole terrible picture. Suddenly I was transported through time, back to my mother's bedroom. All at once, I could see everything, hear everything, feel everything, smell everything. Out loud, in the middle of the service, I suddenly cried, "Oh, my God, it's true!"

I couldn't speak after that, because I couldn't stop crying. In vivid detail, I relived the ugly activity, moment by moment. I realized why so many things about Marla had felt so familiar. I was horrified, devastated. Women came around me to see if they could help, but I couldn't form into words what had just been revealed to me. It was simply too horrible to share.

For three months, I had to take time to grieve over what my mother had done to me. I did not know what to do with all the anger that raged inside me. How could any woman do that to her own daughter? It was all I could do to vocalize it to Ronald. For three months, I could not stand to have anyone, including Ronald, touch me.

Fortunately for me, Ronald was more than patient and understanding. He was frustrated, because it was just one more thing to overcome. I didn't even want him to hug me, but he stood back and told me, "It's okay. Whenever you think you can handle closeness again with me, just let me know. Take whatever time you need." It is amazing to me that he could understand so well, that he could be so loving. His patience allowed me time to deal with these things in my own way.

Meanwhile, I pulled back from being close to anyone. For quite awhile, I wouldn't even let friends lay hands on me to pray.

CHAPTER SIXTEEN

Ronald's advice was to write all my feelings and reactions down on paper and burn it. I did write everything down, but for some reason I did not burn the papers. Those papers, left unburned, became the beginnings of this book.

I could not, would not speak to my mother for two years. I simply couldn't handle it. I wasn't prepared to start the conversation, much less finish it. It didn't have the strength to confront her. I wasn't sure I could forgive her face to face, and I didn't know how she would handle it, either. I could not even call her on the phone.

Over and over again, in obedience to the Lord, I forgave her. For two years, I repeatedly chose to forgive her. But I wasn't sure the forgiveness was permanent. I was afraid that talking with her about what she'd done would break the fragile thread of will power that held me to forgiveness.

It's too bad that I didn't call, because it wasn't long before I found out that my brother, Charlie, had been diagnosed with terminal cancer. I tried every way I could to get Ronald to go with me to New York to stay with my brother for a month, but there was no way for him to be away from work that long. So I had to go alone.

When I arrived in New York, I was devastated to find out that Charlie was gravely ill. My sister, Pat, could not face telling Mom the severity of the diagnosis, so I had to tell her. I was more than apprehensive about seeing my mother again; I didn't know how I'd feel or react to her. I didn't know if I would be able to keep from blowing up or crumbling when I actually saw her again.

But when I got to my mother's house, I suddenly pitied her. She was such a sad, empty, lonely person. There was no pain left in me, no hate, no anger toward her. I felt nothing but sorrow.

I told the truth to both my parents: "Charlie has been diagnosed with stomach cancer. It has more than likely gone into his liver and his pancreas. I don't know how to tell you this, but I don't think he's going to live much longer."

My mother simply looked at me. "That's not true."

FREE INDEED

"Ma, it's true. I don't *want* to tell you this. I haven't seen you in two years. I don't want to tell you this, but it's the truth."

My father started crying, but my mother insisted, without emotion, "It's not true. He's got an ulcer. He'll get over it. He's had ulcers before. It will go away."

No matter what I said, she wouldn't accept it. I just looked at my father. He understood what was happening, and I felt so sorry for him. In his own grief, he would have no support from my mother. She would not accept reality. Outside the house, my father and I cried together in each other's arms for the longest time, until I had to go.

I think that was the beginning of the end for my mother. She couldn't accept losing Charlie. After that, she just seemed to slip in and out of reality.

One day, out of the blue, she said to me, "Did you know that I had twins? They were born dead." Then, the subject changed as though she hadn't said anything about it. I didn't even have the opportunity to ask if they were boys or girls or if they had names. She had slipped back into a dream world. She never mentioned it again. That was the only time I ever heard anything come out of her lips concerning the terrible loss she had experienced when I was just a little girl—a loss that may have changed the course of my life as well as hers. I think the unresolved grief about those babies came back to her as she watched her son die—and it was simply too much for her to handle.

I stayed with my brother for the rest of the month, and talked to him of many things. I told him about my lesbian past. He was very accepting, and not at all shocked. I was surprised to hear him say that he had known; I guess I hadn't kept my secret as well as I thought.

While Charlie was in the hospital, my sister-in-law's minister, Pastor Claudia, came in to visit Charlie. She was the bounciest, bubbliest person either of us had ever seen. She walked into the room one day and introduced herself, then grabbed our hands in hers and said, "Let's pray." She began to pray for Charlie and the family—and then she was off.

CHAPTER SIXTEEN

Charlie looked at me. "Who was that?"

"Pastor Claudia from the church down the street from you. I'm going to church there Sunday. Do you want to go?"

"I think so. She is something else!"

He sat in church that Sunday, prayed, sang, cried, and went to Communion. It blew my mind! He leaned over to me as Communion was being served and asked, "Do you think it will be okay?" I assured him that it would.

We went twice more while I was in New York, and Pastor Claudia came to visit him at home several times while I was there.

I went home in October. In December, I got a call from Pat that Mom was in the hospital with a stroke. In February, another call informed me that Charlie had died. I went back to New York for Charlie's funeral, then went to see my mother in the hospital. She couldn't talk or see anything by that time. No one knew if she understood about Charlie's death.

My brother's funeral was held at Pastor Claudia's church. She told the audience, "I got to know Charlie the past few months. I didn't know him long, but I do know he had a gentle heart, and he had given that heart to the Lord. There's somebody here who needs to know that."

I was so glad that Ronald was with me. And I was so relieved my brother was okay now, and had made the decision to spend his life with the Lord. Still, it was hard to say good-bye.

Within a year of my brother's funeral, my mother also died and I had to endure another trip to New York. I was frightened to go to the wake and see her in the casket. Ronald couldn't come with me this time, and I had to face this particular ordeal alone.

I expected to see the same shriveled, distorted woman whom I remembered. But when I looked into the casket, I blinked in surprise. Somehow, the morticians had made her look young and happy. I couldn't believe my eyes as I saw the most peaceful expression on her face.

I think she must have heard about Charlie going back to church.

She had always worried about him in that regard. In that same moment, I had a revelation in my spirit that her smile was there for another reason: she knew that I had forgiven her of the past. More than anything, I had wanted the opportunity to talk with her and assure her that it was okay, that *I* was okay. Circumstances and fears had kept us from discussing it but now, looking into her face, I knew that she knew. I could see Jesus standing next to her, with His arm around her, pointing down to me, smiling, saying to her, "See? She's okay. She doesn't hate you. She has forgiven all that, and so have I."

For the first time in my life, as I praised the Lord in that church where free expression was very much a part of worship, I knew that my mother was with me. My heart's desire, for so many years, had been to worship with her and the rest of my family. There had never seemed to be an opening or opportunity to discuss the Lord with her; there had been too many barriers in life. But God had sent someone to lead my mother to know and love the Lord, and she had accepted Jesus as her own Lord and Master. Now, as I danced before Jesus, I knew that in heaven Charlie and Ma were dancing with me. Finally we were with the Lord together, one family together in Him.

I was so full of joy that I shocked my family on earth. I wanted to read the scriptures for my mother's funeral service. My sister, Pat, thought I was crazy. "How will you be able to read in front of everyone without falling apart?"

Nevertheless, I stood at the front when it was time for the readings, and I spoke out with joy and confidence. As I stepped down and the service ended, I saw someone at the back of the church. It was Dan, my friend in season and out of season. Standing in the back, to stay out of our family's way, he quietly demonstrated his unqualified love for me.

Dan represented so many countless people whom God wants to reach with healing. There is an entire population of people whose character and spirit, camouflaged by the stony covering of homosexuality, are so precious to Jesus that He will not stop seeking to

CHAPTER SIXTEEN

break apart that covering to set their spirits free. The world sees only the rock-like exterior and passes them by as hopeless. But Jesus, like a master gemologist, sees what is inside. He lines things up, according to His careful eye, and with one careful tap of His anointed hammer of love, cracks the life open. Then all the fire and brilliance hidden inside explodes into dazzling light.

Those who know them, those who have given up on them, are stunned. "How can these things be? We thought we understood."

When the mass was ended, I pulled myself away from my father's and sisters' arms and made my way down that long aisle. I walked past all my relatives, past all our friends, to the back of the church. As I walked, I couldn't help but reminisce about all the things that God had done for me over the years.

He had preserved a young girl from being destroyed by abuse and neglect.

He had restored my uncle to Himself and to me, allowing me to forgive him even before I remembered that there was something to forgive.

He had restored my son to my arms, when it looked like I'd never see him again.

He had restored my brother to Himself, so that death could not steal my childhood companion and friend from me eternally.

He had restored my mother to me, and had implanted the peace that can only come from forgiveness into my heart. When I see her in Glory, I'll see the woman she was always meant to be, and we'll dance together before the Lord.

Over and over again, in my life, God worked gently and persistently in my heart, prodding me to forgive, forgiving things that were humanly unforgivable, helping me repent permanently of the things I never would have imagined I could separate from myself. Today, because of God's power to heal, and to restore, and to forgive, I can remember without remorse, remember without bitterness, remember without pain, and look forward continually to greater and better things.

FREE INDEED

Since that wonderful day of deliverance in New Mexico, I have been busy discovering "Barbara," a woman so discounted and rejected in her youth, that no one had even noticed that I had thrown her away. Since Jesus revealed Himself to me, I continue to discover, with growing awe, that He saw something in me worth spending over fifty years putting back together.

At last I reached the back of the church, where I disappeared into the depths of Dan's arms. "I am so glad you came, Dan. I can't tell you how good it is to see you."

"And I'm so proud of you! You were so amazing up there! I can hardly believe you are the same person I met a few years ago."

I could hardly contain my joy as I responded, "Oh, Dan. Neither can I. God is *so good!*"

Dear Reader,

I've written this book to encourage you that Jesus truly heals lesbianism and homosexuality. There is more available to you than just abstinence, more than struggling with temptation for the rest of your life. Jesus can set you free from every aspect of your unhealthy thought patterns, and from all the junk that goes with them.

Don't be afraid to let Jesus into the painful areas of your life. Allow Him to walk through them with you. With Christ's help, force yourself through the pain.

I know, at times, it is so tempting to try and avoid feeling the pain of the past. When we feel it, the hurt is just as real as if it were happening all over again. But, just think, if you trust Jesus, He can heal that hurt. You will never have to live with that pain again. Just imagine the freedom!

When you push through the past with Jesus Christ, He can heal you forever.

I assure you that He is able to do this.

He did it for me.

Barbara

■ APPENDIX

Resources and Books for Additional Help

ORGANIZATIONS:

Exodus International is a worldwide network of Christian ministries supporting persons seeking to walk out of homosexuality. Services include referrals to local support groups, one-on-one counseling, literature, videos, newsletters and other helpful resources. For a literature packet, contact:

Exodus International
North America
PO Box 77652
Seattle, WA 98177
(206) 784-7799
www.exodusnorthamerica.org

Free Indeed Ministries is a member ministry of Exodus International. Their support group offers help to persons seeking healing from homosexuality, as well as to their friends and family members. Services include a 20-week, closed-group Living Waters Program, referral to other ministries, book lists, tapes, and testimonies. The staff of **Free Indeed** are available for speaking engagements. Contact Ronald or Barbara Swallow at:

Free Indeed Ministries
PO Box 27171
Albuquerque, NM 87125.
(505) 831-5528

AUDIO TAPES:

Exodus International North America produces audiotapes at their annual conference. These tapes deal with issues such as: ex-gay men's issues, ex-lesbian issues, help for friends and family members, counseling, and dealing with AIDS.

For free tape catalogue contact Exodus at (206) 784-7799 or go online to www.cassetteproducts.com.

BOOK LIST:

There are dozens of outstanding books on overcoming homosexuality. Here is a partial listing:

Howard, Jeanette. *Out of Egypt*. Tunbride Wells, England: Monarch, 1991.

Comiskey, Andrew. *Pursuing Sexual Wholeness*. Altamonte Springs, FL: Creation House, 1989.

Dallas, Joe. *Desires in Conflict*. Eugene, OR: Harvest House, 1991.

Payne, Leanne. *The Broken Image*. Wheaton, IL: Crossway Books, 1981.

APPENDIX

Thorkelson-Rentzel, Lori. *Emotional Dependency.* Downers Grove, IL: InterVarsity Press.

Davies, Bob, and Lori Rentzel. *Coming Out of Homosexuality.* Downers Grove, IL: InterVarsity Press, 1993.

Bergner, Mario. *Setting Love in Order.* Grand Rapids, MI: Baker Books, 1995.

Worthen, Anita, and Bob Davies. *Someone I Love is Gay.* Downers Grove, IL: InterVarsity Press, 1996.

There are many other excellent books on the different aspects of overcoming homosexuality and lesbianism. Most are available through your local Christian bookstore. If you prefer, you can also purchase these books by mail order. For a free catalogue of books on homosexuality and related issues, contact:

Regeneration Books
PO Box 9830
Baltimore, MD 21284-9830
(410) 661-4337

or go online to "Resources" at www.exodusnorthamerica.org

WALNUT STREET
METHODIST CHURCH
LIBRARY